FISHING ATLAS FOR PORT PHILLIP BAY & SURROUNDS

AFN™ FISHING & OUTDOORS

JARROD DAY • BILL CLASSON

REX HUNT • STEVE COOPER • MITCH VERTACCINI • LENNY VANDERWAAL • DAVID JARDINE

ACKNOWLEDGEMENTS

Fishing is a past time that all future generations should get to enjoy. Today, we often put work before everything else but times need to change, maybe not for us but for our children and their children. I'm not one to get political but threats of introducing more marine parks, allowing super trawlers into our waterways and banning recreational anglers from fishing certain areas just breaks my heart. In this day and age, politicians should realise that it is recreational anglers that are the best to manage and look after their own fisheries. Sure there are a select minority that break the rules but like in any part of the country, we do have fishery officers, water police, police and the water board to aid in managing those from breaking the law.

When I was a young lad, I may not have been interested in school; in fact fishing took centre stage and it was all I could think about. Every Christmas holiday, a family friend by the name of Lou, took me fishing out from Sorrento on his yacht. We'd drift the Sorrento channel for flathead and come home with a bucket load. Those were the days and now some thirty years on, still reminisce of those memories I'll never forget.

Work life can change this in a heart beat and it is up to us parents to get our kids into fishing. Not just to teach them how to fish but to spend time together and hopefully one day, they too will be standing up to defend their local fishery should politics still be one of those deciding factors of who gets the vote.

That aside, for me, fishing was something I always thrived on. From the ripe old age of 6 sitting on the Sorrento caravan park jetty catching flathead too my adolescent years of fishing the entire Mornington peninsula on foot, I have no-one more to thank than my Nan for giving me the freedom to explore the beaches with my rod and reel in hand.

A lifetime of Rex Hunt on the Television, Kai Bush (Bushy), Steve Starling (Starlo), Paul Worsteling, Lee Rainer, Andrew Ettingshausen (ET) and Alistair McGlashan have followed on from where Rex left off.

Today's pinnacle of TV hosts that have continued to put fishing on the map and have dedicated their lives to fishing and encouraging the younger generation to also be involved in such a relaxing and enjoyable sport.

To those people of some I personally know well I thank you, you are the ones that gave me the mindset that fishing is fun.

Along the journey, I cut my teeth fishing with some really close mates that took the next step to run their own fishing charters businesses.

Simon Rinaldi from Red Hot Fishing Charters, Matt Cini from Reel Time Fishing Charters, Matt Boultin from Fishing On Charters, Frank Milito From East Gippsland Charters, Mitch Bertachinni from Online Fishing Charters amongst a stack of other great mates I have met along they way both on Australian soil and aboard, these guys are the offspring of their fathers, another generation of anglers we only hear about in past stories past down from angler to angler.

While there are too many people to mention individually, without the help of everyone I have met over the years, this book would have never made it to print, for that, I thank you.

To my wife and children, you are the best. Many people have asked me where to find a wife that is so understanding to let me go fishing at any time day or night and my answer is simple, you can't, I got her.

On that note, fishing for some is a time to escape the daily activities of life and to others it is a few hours to sit back, relax and enjoy being outside. For me, it is a passion within and something that I just can't give up doing. Fishing has taken me too many places, in fact throughout the majority of Australia and many international destinations. I have met a lot of people in the past two decades and have enjoyed every second of it.

First published 2017, Reprint 2026

Published by AFN Fishing & Outdoors
Australian Fishing Network
PO Box 544 Croydon, Victoria 3136
Telephone: (03) 9729 8788 Email: sales@afn.com.au
www.afn.com.au

ISBN: 9781 8651 3293 8

Printed in China

FOREWORD

Melbourne certainly is a special place and with Port Phillip Bay and it's tributaries on the CBD's back door step, it is no wonder why so many Victorian's enjoy recreational fishing as a hobby.

There are no rules in fishing, you are always learning and no matter how much you think you know, there is always still more.

Port Phillip Bay and its tributaries are forever changing and whether it is environmental factors causing a change or through state, federal or local council we need to be kept up to speed with everything that is going on.

Staying up to date is not always that easy, however with the power of social media in today's era, new rules and regulations are more easily obtainable than ever before.

Saltwater fishing in Port Phillip Bay thrives on the annual snapper migration and despite having its ups and downs; it is still the biggest drawcard to recreational fishing in the state.

Port Phillip Bay has gone through many things, the abolishment of scallop dredging, dredging the bay so larger ships can enter non-fishing ship transit lanes and still to this day, the fishing is consistent each season.

Over the coming years, netting will be banned in the Bay and while long lining for snapper will continue, I can only see our fishery getting better for the future.

Fishing the Bay is not just about the snapper fishery though, calamari, king George whiting, garfish, gummy shark, leather jacket, flathead, kingfish, warehou and a host of other species are a viable option at different times of the year.

Port Phillip Bay is a paradise and though it might not have coral reefs and temperate waters, it is a place the entire family can enjoy every day of the year.

There is much to learn when fishing the Bay so take your time and learn by listening to others.

Don't go out hoping to catch a fish, rather expect to catch one. Do this by learning about each species. Where it lives, what it eats, when it is abundant and everything else that you can find out. The more you know about a particular species, the more chance you have at catching it.

There is a lot of information within the pages of this book, most of which has taken myself two decades of learning and listening from others as well as teaching myself by putting in time on the water.

Regardless of how often you fish or where you fish, there is just one rule to stand by, fishing is about having fun and enjoying yourself.

Jarrod Day

Safety Disclaimer

Information published in this book should be used as a guide only. Maps and GPS coordinates should not be used for navigational purposes. Water depths shown on maps have been thoroughly reviewed at the time of publication but cannot be guaranteed. The changing nature of the marine environment suggests that some structures are likely to change in response to the forces of nature. Mariners should use the latest information available to plan safe passage through the waters described in this book. Published GPS coordinates have been obtained from reliable sources and although every effort was made, not all were able to be verified. These marks cannot be guaranteed.

CONTENTS

NAVIGATION AIDS FOR MAPS

Port When lighted exhibits   Starboard When lighted exhibits

Beacons, Bouys

CARDINAL MARKS Indicate navigable water for the area beyond the mark in the direction depicted.

North

West

East

South

Lighted marks all exhibit a WHITE light.

SPECIAL MARKS Indicate several features (eg: pipe outfall) where navigable water is usually evident from the map.

When lighted exhibits

ISOLATED DANGER MARKS Are stationed over a submerged hazard. KEEP CLEAR.

When lighted exhibits

SAFE WATER MARKS

When lighted exhibits

MARINE PARK BUOYS

GPS MARKS ◎

SCALE FOR MAPS 1-16

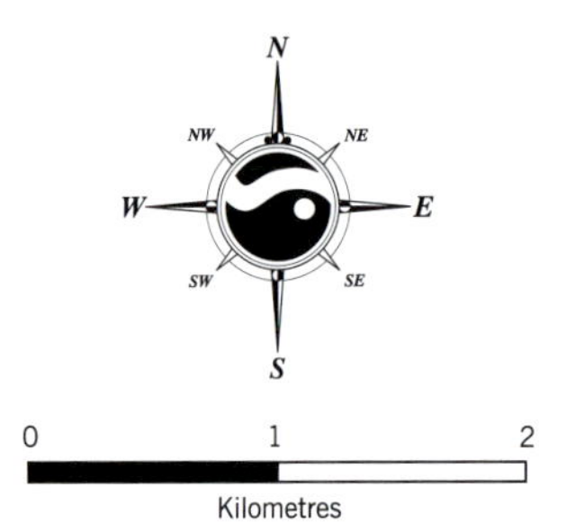

KEY FOR MAPS

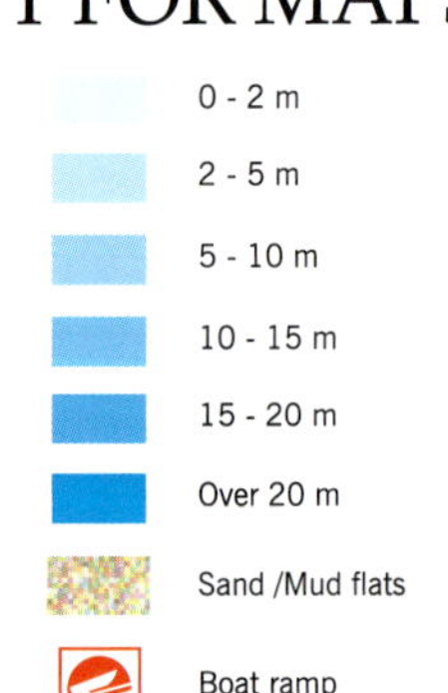

KEY MAP Locations of Maps for Port Phillip Bay & Surrounds

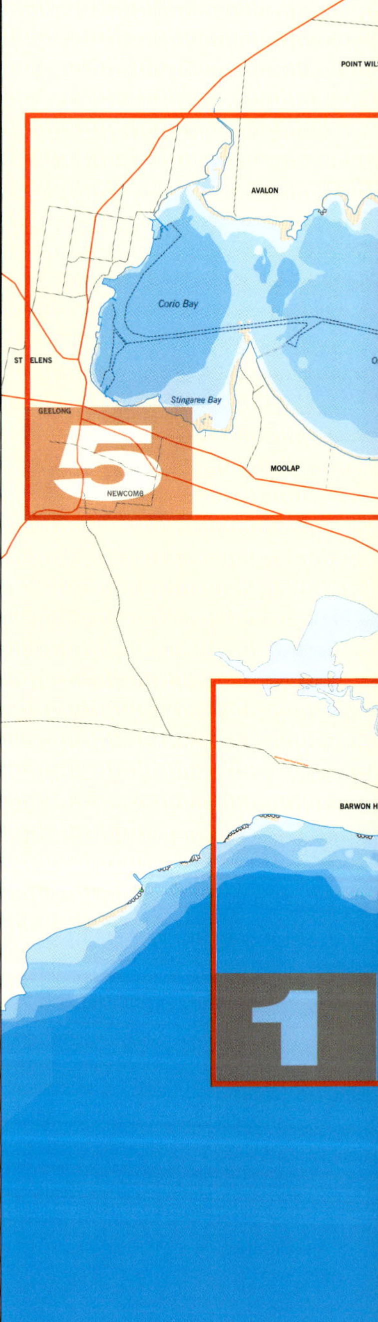

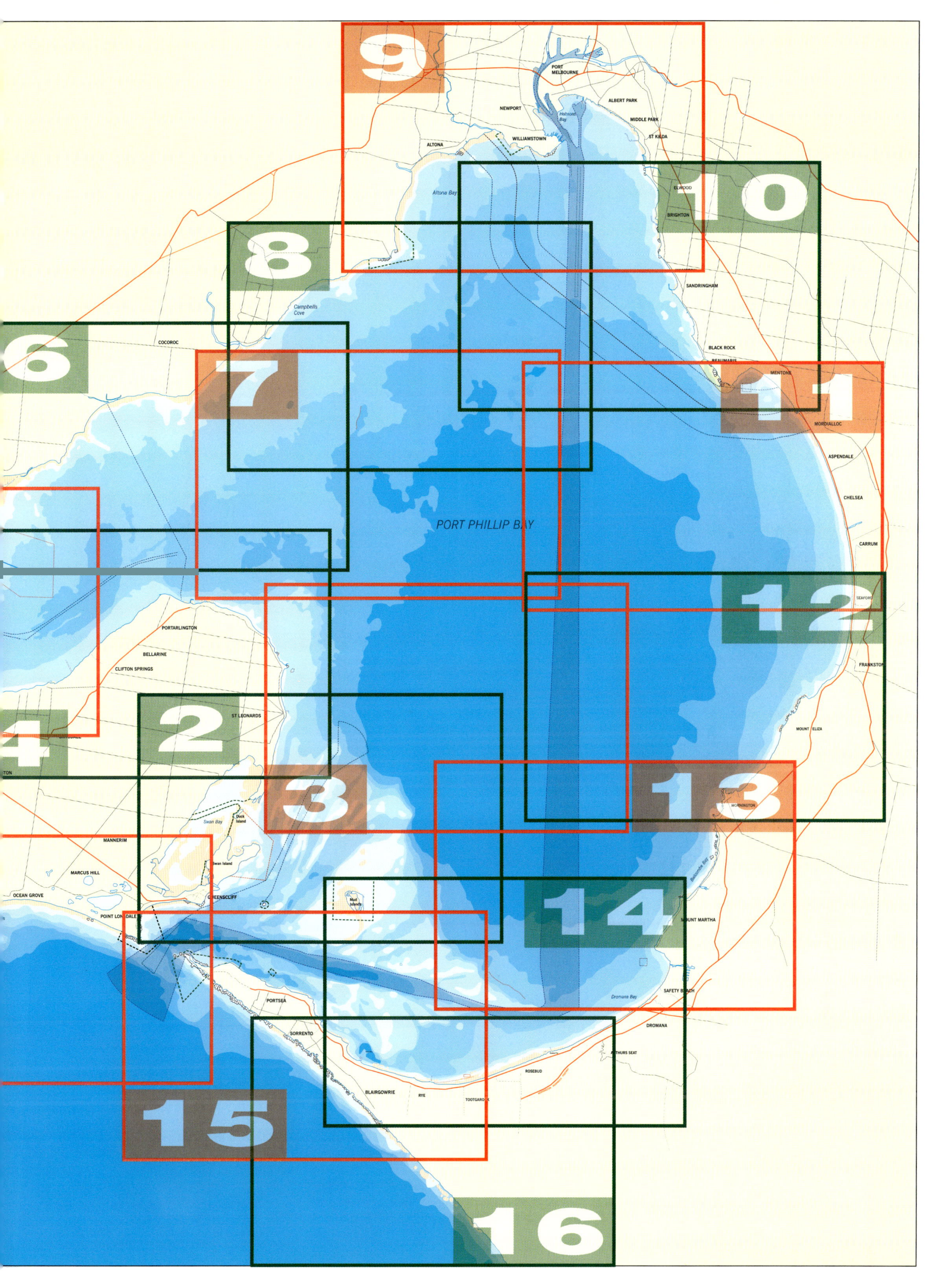
9
PORT MELBOURNE
ALBERT PARK
NEWPORT
Hobsons Bay
MIDDLE PARK
ST KILDA
WILLIAMSTOWN
ALTONA
Altona Bay
10
ELWOOD
BRIGHTON
8
SANDRINGHAM
Campbells Cove
6
COCOROC
BLACK ROCK
BEAUMARIS
7
MENTONE
11
MORDIALLOC
ASPENDALE
CHELSEA
PORT PHILLIP BAY
CARRUM
SEAFORD
12
PORTARLINGTON
BELLARINE
CLIFTON SPRINGS
FRANKSTON
2
ST LEONARDS
4
MOUNT ELIZA
3
13
MORNINGTON
Swan Bay
Duck Island
MANNERIM
Swan Island
MARCUS HILL
OCEAN GROVE
QUEENSCLIFF
Mud Islands
POINT LONSDALE
14
MOUNT MARTHA
Balcombe Bay
SAFETY BEACH
Dromana Bay
PORTSEA
DROMANA
SORRENTO
ARTHURS SEAT
ROSEBUD
BLAIRGOWRIE
RYE
TOOTGAROOK
15
16

PART ONE
PORT PHILLIP BAY

Mornington Pier on Sunrise, a great time to catch southern calamari.

Shaped like a big bowl, the 1200 square kilometres of Port Phillip Bay is surrounded by the majority of the Victorian population, who use it for all manner of purposes: for recreation like fishing, diving, sailing, swimming; through to commercial activities like sea freight and commercial fishing.

Thankfully in a day and age where the majority of changes are for the worst, it's great to see that our bay has never been in better shape. This is thanks in large part to the actions of a dedicated and concerned group of anglers, who back in 1996, marched on Parliament house to get the message across to then Premier Jeff Kennett and his government to stop the scallop dredges from destroying the bay.

In the relatively short time since, the water clarity in the bay has become better than ever. What reef systems there are have abundant growth on them. With such a good environment we are seeing the benefits in the form of several of the best snapper seasons ever recorded. Snapper migrate into the bay each year, and there isn't a fish that is more famous or creates more excitement each spring. The snapper come on mass to feed and spawn over the relatively barren mud bottom that makes up much of the bay. For the majority of anglers fishing in the bay they are the ultimate prize. Snapper can be targeted from the shore or from a boat, and using a variety of different methods ranging from fishing with live or dead bait, to the exciting method of fishing with soft plastic lures.

Aside from the snapper, there are a host of other species on offer at various times in the bay, like whiting, flathead, garfish, salmon, snook, red mullet, gummy sharks, trevally, bream and even yellowtail kingfish.

Best of all, within the confines of this one circular body of water, the bay presents a variety of locations that offer totally different fishing conditions.

In covering Port Phillip Bay, maps on pages 8–39 will assist you in locating some of the more productive spots. However these maps are only intended as a guide to finding fishing spots and proper admiralty charts should be used for navigation purposes.

CHAPTER 1
BARWON HEADS TO POINT LONSDALE
MAP 1

The stretch of water from Barwon Heads to Point Lonsdale is our starting point in a clockwise direction around Port Phillip Bay. The water offshore from Barwon Heads is home to some good reef systems that hold snapper and gummy sharks, while trolling in close often produces salmon, snook and more than the occasional kingfish. The Barwon River Estuary consists of a narrow of a narrow entrance to the sea, with minimal siltation, a broad-water extending about 2.5 km upstream from the bridge, and a long winding section of about 4 or 5 km up to Lake Connewarre.

Ocean Grove Beach is a Shallow featureless beach that produces good results throughout the year for snapper and mulloway. Collendina is also a shallow, unattractive beach at first glance, but can produce snapper and mulloway for prepared anglers.

Thirteenth Beach

Thirteenth Beach runs west from Barwon Bluff to the sewerage outfall at Black Rocks. The beach is interspersed with reef and the gutters adjacent provide the best opportunities for catching salmon, snapper and a good many other fish. However it is very exposed, which makes it hard to get out of the weather when it comes from the south, though it does produce good fishing. As well as the gutters, the shallow washes hold great numbers of small mullet and juvenile salmon, so all you need is a little berley in the form of tuna soaked pellets and small baits such as pilchard fillet, peeled prawn or pipi.

Larger baits fished in close proximity to some of the rock and reef often produce larger salmon, while at night, anglers take a few gummy sharks along with the occasional mulloway, captures of which are kept very quiet.

Charlemont Reef

About 1 km out from Thirteenth Beach is the highest point on the West Bank called Charlemont Reef. It breaks heavily in any kind of a swell so should be avoided at those times. On a good day, fish close to the reef to catch a wide variety of fish such as, pike, snook, salmon and trevally on both bait and lures. This area has also been producing some good sized kingfish by trolling live baits such as calamari, salmon and yellowtail. Flicking soft plastics when the fish are on the surface can be a lot of fun. If the kingfish are down deep, anglers can use metal jigs in the 200-250 g weight range which is also highly effective along the edges of the reef.

A local fishing charter works a school of salmon on the edge of Charlemont Reef.

Mako Sharks are abundant offshore.

Barwon Bluff

Good catches of salmon are made regularly about 500 m out from the bluff by anglers trolling with lures. Around to the right of the bluff about 300 m out, is an excellent place to catch sweep by setting a berley trail of mashed pilchards to get the sweep into a feeding frenzy. Unweighted baits can then be sent down the trail.

It is often dangerous to cut to the right in front of the bluff when leaving the river as waves can break without warning. Maintain your heading until well clear of the bluff.

Ocean Grove Beach

Although fish have been caught at all stages of all the tides both during the day and night, fishing the beach on a low tide is recommended when the angler can wade out far enough to be able to cast into productive water. Evening low tides in late spring and summer and daybreak in autumn and winter give the best fishing opportunities here.

A running sinker rig or paternoster rig will work well in this location. Live baiting salmon is effective for mulloway, especially on the lead up to a full moon. Include star sinkers to 7 oz in your gear as from time to time strong currents can make fishing difficult.

Collendina

Low tide seems to be the best time, and the best places to fish are adjacent to the obvious exposed patches of reef at either end of the beach. Long casts are required to reach the desired distance to where snapper may be holding.

As with all the beaches close to Port Phillip Heads, the most common fish are small salmon and good sized mullet. These can be caught on light tackle in the wash particularly at low tide. A paternoster rig tied from 10 lb fluorocarbon leader with two droppers each containing a size #8 or #10 long shank works best. Both species take a variety of baits but pipi is favoured over all.

There are some other big fish lurking about in this area, so it is worth putting out a larger bait of salmon or mullet fillets especially if fishing the beach at night.

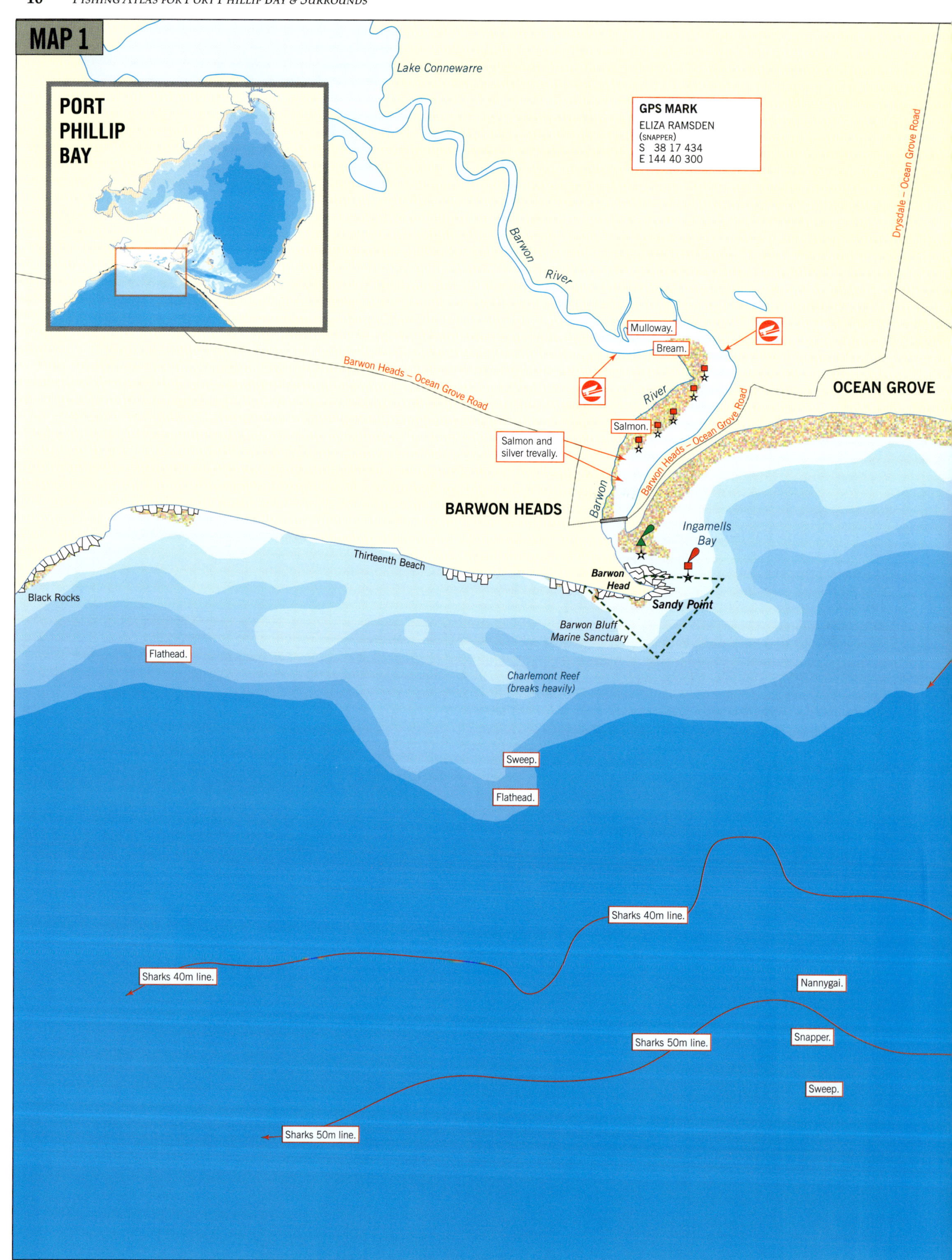
MAP 1
PORT PHILLIP BAY
Lake Connewarre
GPS MARK
ELIZA RAMSDEN
(SNAPPER)
S 38 17 434
E 144 40 300
Drysdale – Ocean Grove Road
Barwon River
Mulloway.
Bream.
Barwon Heads – Ocean Grove Road
River
OCEAN GROVE
Salmon.
Salmon and silver trevally.
Barwon Heads – Ocean Grove Road
Barwon
BARWON HEADS
Ingamells Bay
Thirteenth Beach
Barwon Head
Sandy Point
Black Rocks
Barwon Bluff Marine Sanctuary
Flathead.
Charlemont Reef (breaks heavily)
Sweep.
Flathead.
Sharks 40m line.
Sharks 40m line.
Nannygai.
Sharks 50m line.
Snapper.
Sweep.
Sharks 50m line.

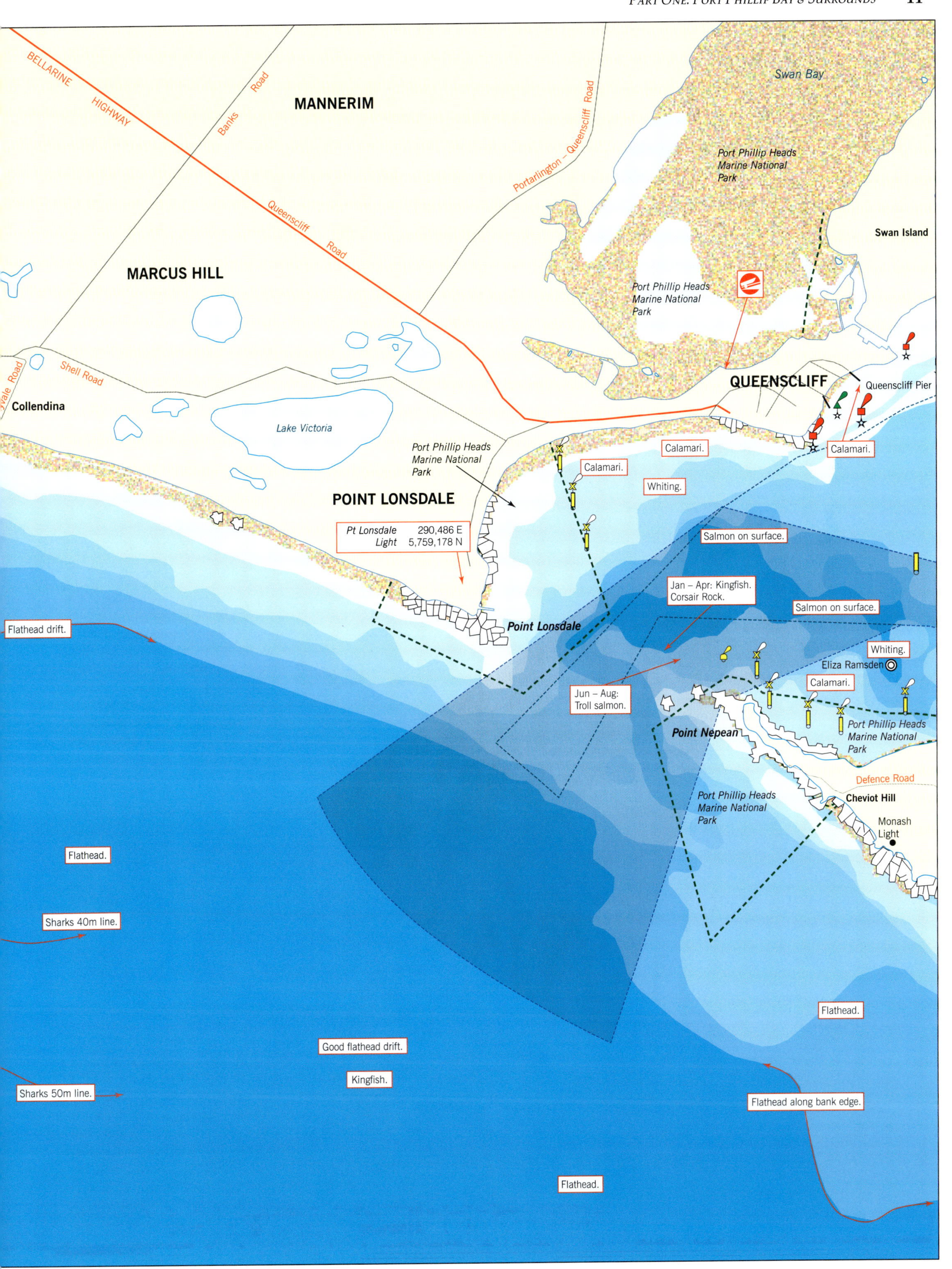

BELLARINE HIGHWAY
Banks Road
MANNERIM
Portarlington – Queenscliff Road
Swan Bay
Port Phillip Heads Marine National Park
Queenscliff Road
MARCUS HILL
Swan Island
Port Phillip Heads Marine National Park
Shell Road
Collendina
QUEENSCLIFF
Queenscliff Pier
Lake Victoria
Port Phillip Heads Marine National Park
Calamari.
Calamari.
Calamari.
Whiting.
POINT LONSDALE
Pt Lonsdale Light 290,486 E 5,759,178 N
Salmon on surface.
Jan – Apr: Kingfish. Corsair Rock.
Salmon on surface.
Flathead drift.
Point Lonsdale
Whiting.
Eliza Ramsden
Calamari.
Jun – Aug: Troll salmon.
Point Nepean
Port Phillip Heads Marine National Park
Defence Road
Port Phillip Heads Marine National Park
Cheviot Hill
Monash Light
Flathead.
Sharks 40m line.
Flathead.
Good flathead drift.
Kingfish.
Sharks 50m line.
Flathead along bank edge.
Flathead.

CHAPTER 2
POINT LONSDALE TO PORTARLINGTON
MAPS 2, 3 & 4

Point Lonsdale

Although surrounded by the Port Phillip Heads Marine National Park, fishing is permitted for a distance of 50 m either side of the Point Lonsdale Pier. The pier does not produce the catches of fish one might expect considering the location. However, it does fish moderately well for salmon on a rising tide. Best results are usually in the early mornings when salmon will readily take a lure.

Big whiting are also caught from half way up the pier during the evening after a hot day. Garfish are a worthy target and can be attracted in large schools. Due to the proximity of the pier to the ocean, these garfish can be of exceptional size.

From September to late October, Snapper can also be taken from the pier both during the day and night. Sometimes there are big fish among these.

A variety of sharks including seven gill, gummy and bronze whalers, can be caught from the pier during February if the angler is equipped with game fishing tackle. Large balloons or floats are necessary to deploy the large baits (usually tuna) when the wind is offshore, but be aware of the park boundary.

The Kelp Patch

The kelp patch is a kilometre offshore from Clarkes Beacon, which is on the shore about half way between Queenscliff and Point Lonsdale. Easy to find with the long tendrils of kelp reaching the surface of the water. Trolling here produces a variety of predatory fish including salmon and snook, and the occasional kingfish.

Just inside the kelp patch excellent catches of big whiting are sometimes taken and garfish will respond to berleying. Squid are also here in good numbers.

Be aware that the marine park is immediately south of Clarkes Beacon and where fishing is prohibited.

Bell Reef

This rock formation underneath the white lighthouse on Shortland Bluff is exposed at low tide. A favourite spot for squid, it also does produce other species as well, particularly small flathead from the north end. Anglers casting from this north end adjacent to the beacon have also taken snapper. A baited squid-jig fished on rod and reel is the favoured technique of catching squid from this ledge because hand lining is difficult.

Good catches of silver trevally have been taken here during the day in October and November, while on evening, from September through to mid-November, good sized snapper can be caught by using freshly caught squid for bait. Yellowtail Kingfish have also been hooked from this ledge with freshly caught squid of generous proportions, but most of these either get away or have been broken off on purpose mistaken for a stingray.

In summer, the low tides from late afternoon to dusk are most suitable for the angler as the tide is lower than the morning low tides that sometimes barely expose the platform at all.

Queenscliff Boat Harbour and Ramp

The boat ramp and harbour are both inside the narrow southern entrance to Swan Bay, which is a shallow tidal lagoon some five nautical miles in length by 2 miles across. Anglers must acquaint themselves with the boundary of the Swan Bay part of the Port Phillip Heads Marine National Park where fishing is prohibited.

Swan Bay is only navigable for a short distance from the

Queenscliff is a popular location to drift for calamari. When they are abundant a lot of anglers take the opportunity to catch them.

Artificial jigs work extremely well on calamari.

Queenscliff ramp, but good catches of silver trevally can be made inside the harbour near the ramp, particularly on the incoming tide. From a boat, the best place to fish is between the yacht club and the bridge, but keep out of the channel and beware of the large commercial fishing boats.

Boats of up to 7 m can be launched from the ramp at the bottom of Hesse Street which is adequately sheltered in all conditions except a very strong northerly wind.

Landbased anglers can fish from the entrance wall near the ferry terminal and from wharves and structures inside the harbour for mullet and silver trevally.

Queenscliff Pier

Small flathead, garfish, leatherjacket and squid are the main species caught from the Queenscliff Pier.

Garfish are targeted when the current is running out so that the float is drawn away from the pier in the berley trail. Leatherjacket are regularly caught down around the pylons using fresh squid or pipis on long-shanked hooks as these fish can bite through the line. Good quantities of squid are taken from the pier, but the best catches are taken at night halfway along the pier. Look for the ink stains on the pier for the choice spots to catch your squid.

Lure casting from the pier at daybreak can produce a salmon or two, but after sunrise your chances will have faded. Fishing the bottom will produce a variety of fish, but small flathead predominate.

For those in the know and who have specialised techniques, sharks can also be caught from the pier.

The White Lady

This is the name given to the prominent Coles Channel Marker off the northern tip of Swan Island. North and east of this marker, good catches of whiting are made, particularly during the ebb tide. About 400 m to the east of this marker, the bottom drops away into the blind fork of the West Channel. In the spring, good catches of snapper are taken along this drop-off.

Swan Bay Entrance

Queenscliff Harbour is the south entrance to Swan Bay, but the recognised entrance for navigation purposes is between Duck Island and Point Edwards some 3 or 4 km to the north-west of Coles Beacon. The channel forks in two and the lesser channel runs close in to the north end of Duck Island from where you can fish from the shore, particularly at the very bottom of the tide when eel grass is not such a problem. Here you are likely to catch good size gummy sharks. Other species like snapper and mulloway have been caught here too, but not very often. On warm days, big flathead bask on the shallow banks just inside the entrance, particularly in December, January and February.

To catch these fish, it is best to anchor up in the shallows in less than a metre of water, then drift a whitebait down the tide about half a metre under a float. If a flathead is on your drift, you will pick him up. If you have no success after a couple of tries, up-anchor and move somewhere else, but not into deep water. Calamari are a good target on the banks of the entrance. The weed beds here are quite extensive, supporting a good calamari population throughout the year. From September to November, big spawning calamari can be found.

Swan Bay

The vast majority of Swan Bay is part of the Port Phillip Heads Marine National Park and fishing is prohibited. Anglers should check the Parks Victoria website for details of the very limited area still open to fishing.

St Leonards

The St Leonards boat ramp at the end of Leviens Road is badly exposed to an onshore breeze or swell, and rocks in the water are a potential hazard. However, under favourable conditions, craft to 5 m can be launched and retrieved.

St Leonards Pier

The pier at St Leonards has gained a deserved reputation for producing both snapper (to those who are prepared to put in the time) and squid. Sadly, the wooden decking over the rock breakwater has been removed and the breakwater itself is an unsafe fishing platform.

Indented Head

There is an adequate boat launching facility at Indented Head, but nowhere for landbased anglers to fish with any expectation of success. The St Leonards Pier nearby is a better proposition.

The Governor Reefs, clearly marked with isolated danger marks and cardinal marks, and all within a kilometre or so of the Indented Head ramp, are good whiting and squid grounds, principally because they are difficult for commercial fishermen to net so consequently retain good populations of fish.

This area is also the best location to catch whiting throughout the winter months. Work the sand holes for the best results. Calamari are in abundance over the weed beds year round. Size 3.0 jigs are best offered.

Grassy Point

Grassy Point is one of the best known whiting producing areas on the Bellarine Peninsula, although it does get a hiding from commercial fish harvesting operations. The boat ramp at Grassy Point offers marginal access for small to medium boats although it is difficult at low tide.

Whiting are usually plentiful at the edge of the mussel leases where they can't be netted, and squid are usually small but prolific. Over the grass beds throughout. Get in close and set a berley trail to coax the fish to your location. A paternoster rig will work best here. Best baits include pipi and mussel.

Steeles Rocks

Adjacent to the small boat ramp at the bottom of Fairfax Street, Steeles Rocks provide a marginal platform for anglers seeking squid and whiting. Being able to cast well out with light tackle is an advantage when seeking whiting here.

Yabbies may be pumped from the muddy sand between the Portarlington Pier and Steeles Rocks provided the tide goes out far enough to expose their holes.

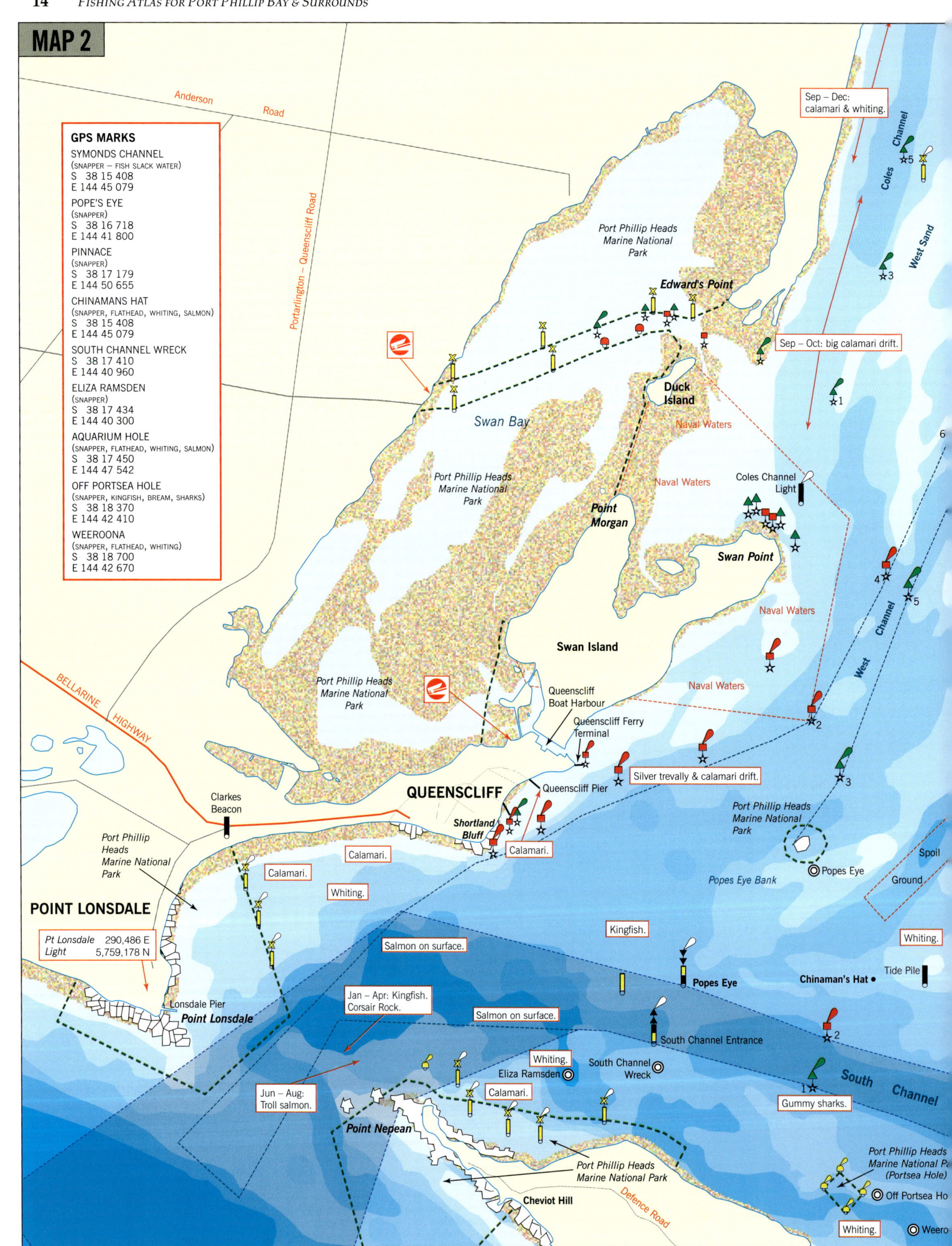
MAP 2
GPS MARKS
SYMONDS CHANNEL
(SNAPPER – FISH SLACK WATER)
S 38 15 408
E 144 45 079
POPE'S EYE
(SNAPPER)
S 38 16 718
E 144 41 800
PINNACE
(SNAPPER)
S 38 17 179
E 144 50 655
CHINAMANS HAT
(SNAPPER, FLATHEAD, WHITING, SALMON)
S 38 15 408
E 144 45 079
SOUTH CHANNEL WRECK
S 38 17 410
E 144 40 960
ELIZA RAMSDEN
(SNAPPER)
S 38 17 434
E 144 40 300
AQUARIUM HOLE
(SNAPPER, FLATHEAD, WHITING, SALMON)
S 38 17 450
E 144 47 542
OFF PORTSEA HOLE
(SNAPPER, KINGFISH, BREAM, SHARKS)
S 38 18 370
E 144 42 410
WEEROONA
(SNAPPER, FLATHEAD, WHITING)
S 38 18 700
E 144 42 670
Anderson Road
Portarlington – Queenscliff Road
BELLARINE HIGHWAY
Sep – Dec: calamari & whiting.
Coles Channel
West Sand
Port Phillip Heads Marine National Park
Edward's Point
Sep – Oct: big calamari drift.
Duck Island
Swan Bay
Naval Waters
Coles Channel Light
Point Morgan
Swan Point
Swan Island
West Channel
Queenscliff Boat Harbour
Queenscliff Ferry Terminal
Silver trevally & calamari drift.
Queenscliff Pier
QUEENSCLIFF
Clarkes Beacon
Shortland Bluff
Calamari.
Whiting.
Popes Eye
Popes Eye Bank
Spoil Ground
POINT LONSDALE
Pt Lonsdale Light 290,486 E 5,759,178 N
Lonsdale Pier
Point Lonsdale
Kingfish.
Salmon on surface.
Whiting.
Tide Pile
Chinaman's Hat
Jan – Apr: Kingfish. Corsair Rock.
South Channel Entrance
Eliza Ramsden
South Channel Wreck
Jun – Aug: Troll salmon.
Point Nepean
South Channel
Gummy sharks.
Port Phillip Heads Marine National Park (Portsea Hole)
Off Portsea Ho
Cheviot Hill
Defence Road
Weero

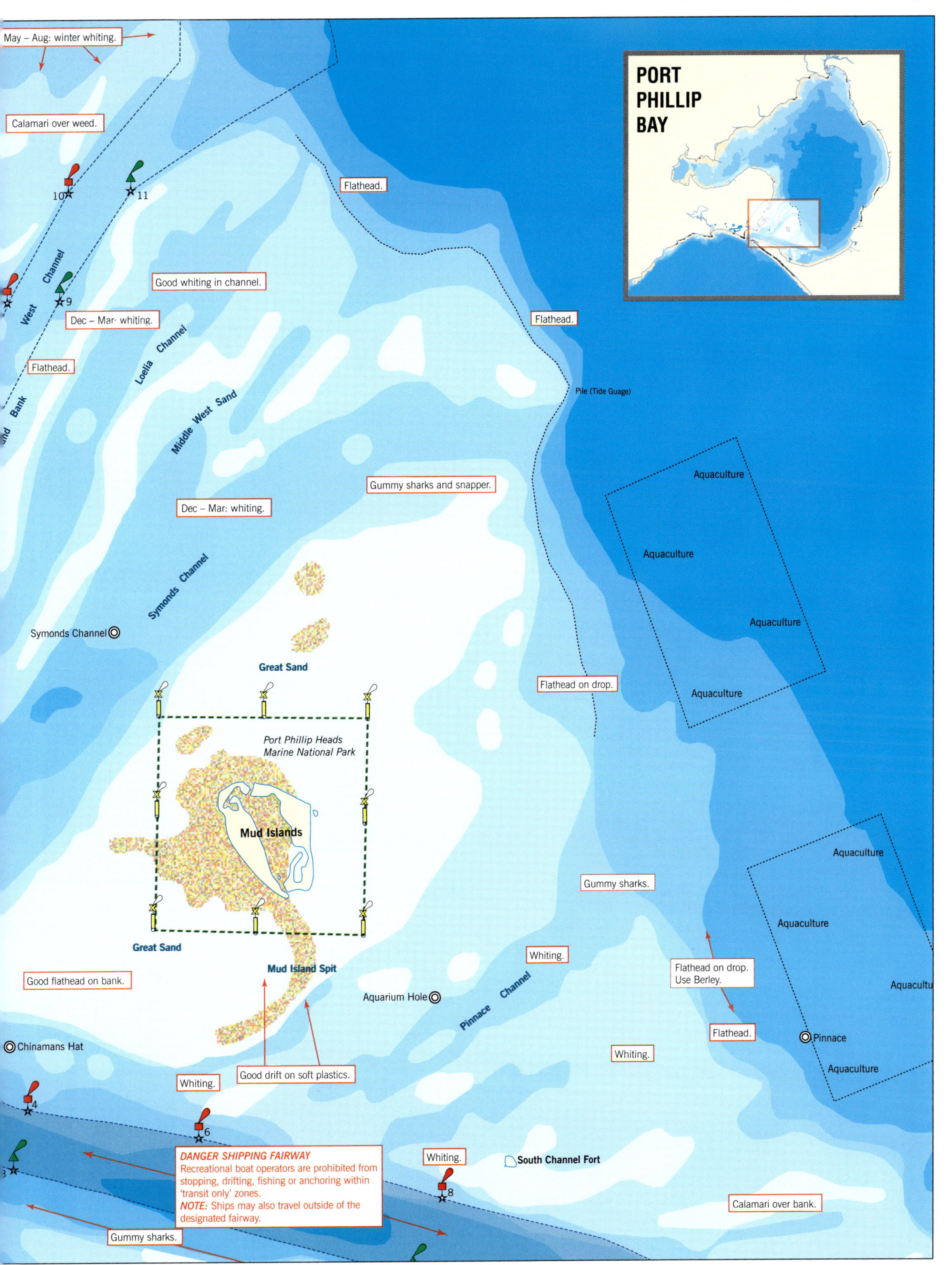
PORT PHILLIP BAY
May – Aug: winter whiting.
Calamari over weed.
Flathead.
Good whiting in channel.
Dec – Mar: whiting.
Flathead.
West Channel
Loelia Channel
Middle West Sand
Flathead.
Pile (Tide Guage)
Gummy sharks and snapper.
Dec – Mar: whiting.
Symonds Channel
Symonds Channel
Aquaculture
Aquaculture
Aquaculture
Aquaculture
Great Sand
Flathead on drop.
Port Phillip Heads Marine National Park
Mud Islands
Gummy sharks.
Aquaculture
Aquaculture
Great Sand
Whiting.
Mud Island Spit
Flathead on drop. Use Berley.
Good flathead on bank.
Aquarium Hole
Pinnace Channel
Flathead.
Pinnace
Chinamans Hat
Whiting.
Aquaculture
Whiting.
Good drift on soft plastics.
DANGER SHIPPING FAIRWAY
Recreational boat operators are prohibited from stopping, drifting, fishing or anchoring within 'transit only' zones.
NOTE: Ships may also travel outside of the designated fairway.
Whiting.
South Channel Fort
Calamari over bank.
Gummy sharks.

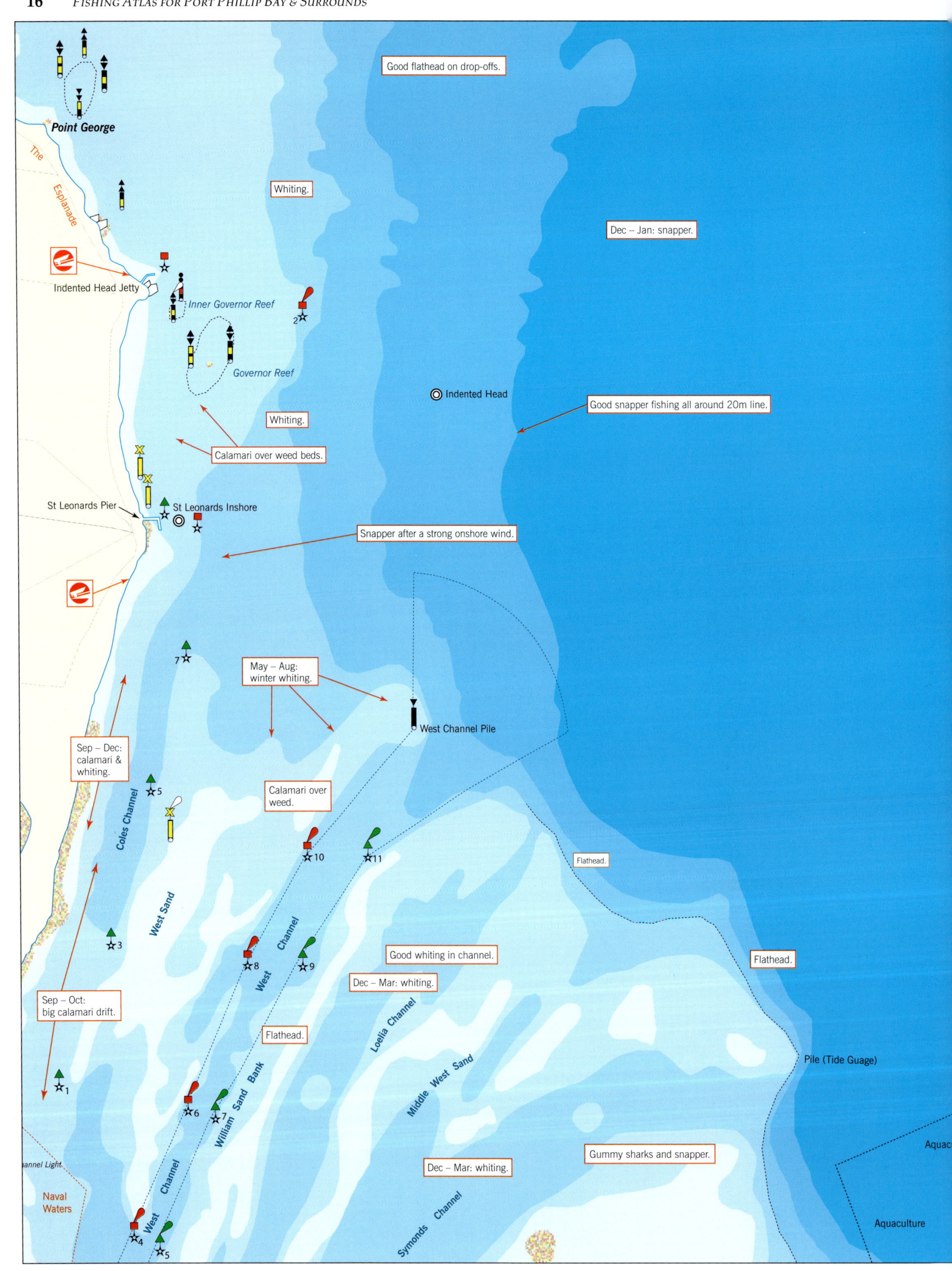

Point George
The Esplanade
Good flathead on drop-offs.
Whiting.
Dec – Jan: snapper.
Indented Head Jetty
Inner Governor Reef
Governor Reef
Indented Head
Good snapper fishing all around 20m line.
Whiting.
Calamari over weed beds.
St Leonards Pier
St Leonards Inshore
Snapper after a strong onshore wind.
May – Aug: winter whiting.
West Channel Pile
Sep – Dec: calamari & whiting.
Calamari over weed.
Coles Channel
Flathead.
West Sand
West Channel
Good whiting in channel.
Flathead.
Dec – Mar: whiting.
Sep – Oct: big calamari drift.
Flathead.
Loelia Channel
Pile (Tide Guage)
William Sand Bank
Middle West Sand
Naval Waters
West Channel
Gummy sharks and snapper.
Dec – Mar: whiting.
Symonds Channel
Aquaculture

MAP 3

PORT PHILLIP BAY

DANGER SHIPPING FAIRWAY
Recreational boat operators are prohibited from stopping, drifting, fishing or anchoring within 'transit only' zones.
NOTE: Ships may also travel outside of the designated fairway.

Deep mackerel (21m) and excellent snapper.

Excellent snapper. Sound to locate.

GPS MARKS

ST LEONARDS INSHORE (5M SNAPPER)
S 38 10 177
E 144 43 608

INDENTED HEAD (SNAPPER)
S 38 08 200
E 144 45 340

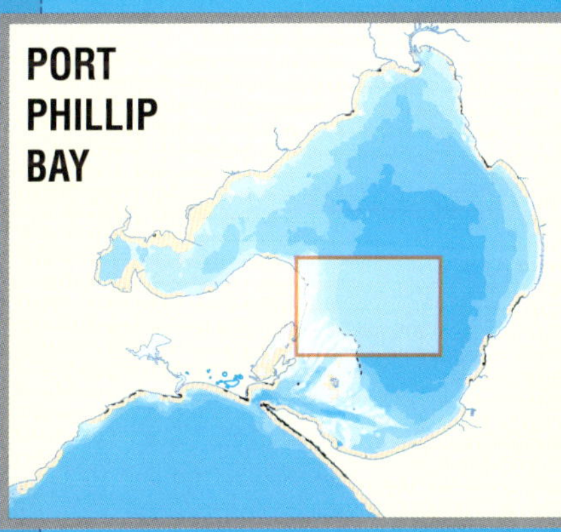

Excellent snapper.

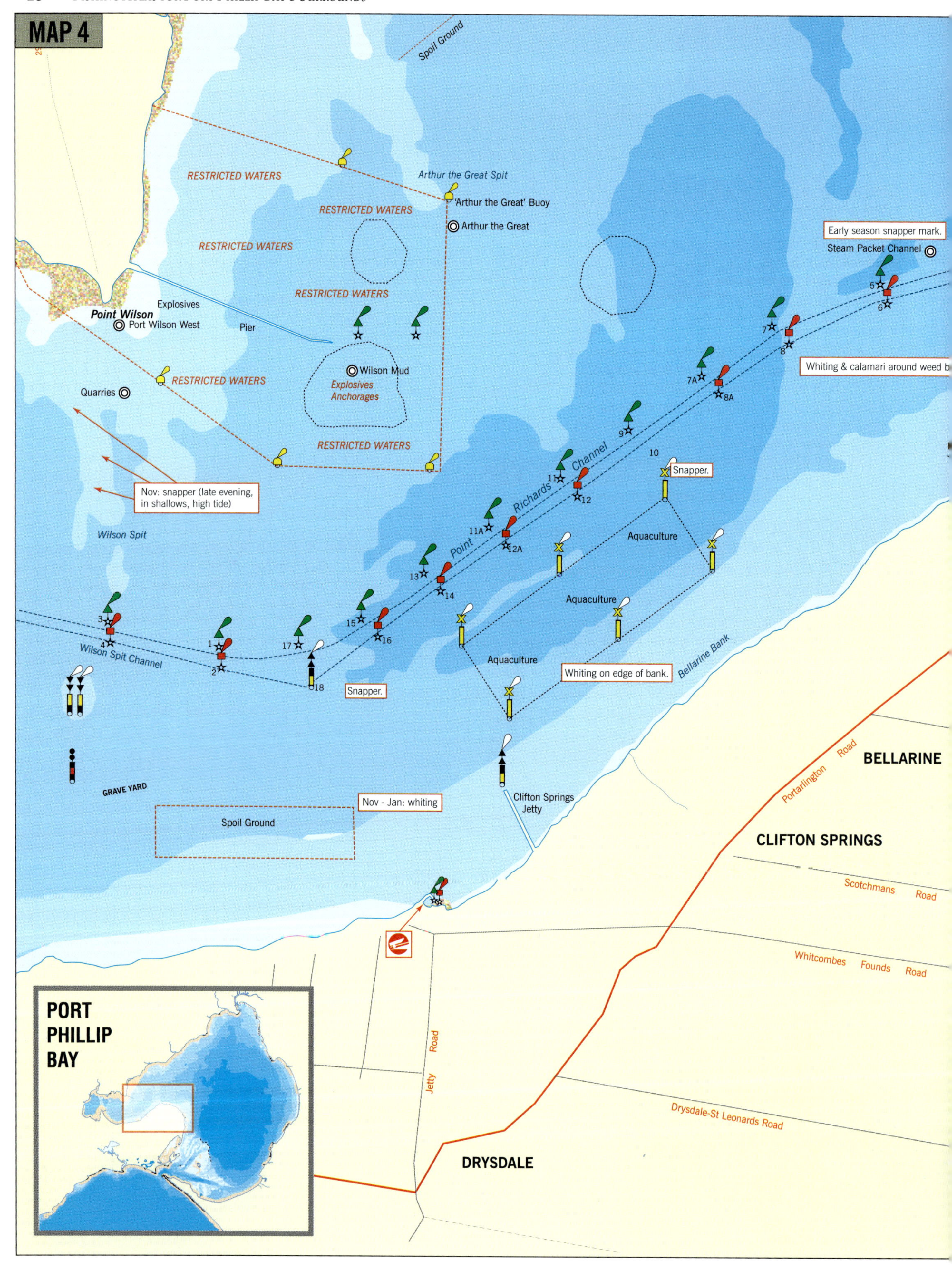
MAP 4
Spoil Ground
RESTRICTED WATERS
Arthur the Great Spit
'Arthur the Great' Buoy
Arthur the Great
RESTRICTED WATERS
RESTRICTED WATERS
Early season snapper mark.
Steam Packet Channel
RESTRICTED WATERS
Explosives
Point Wilson
Port Wilson West
Pier
Wilson Mud
Explosives Anchorages
Whiting & calamari around weed b
Quarries
RESTRICTED WATERS
RESTRICTED WATERS
Point Richards Channel
Snapper.
Nov: snapper (late evening, in shallows, high tide)
Wilson Spit
Aquaculture
Aquaculture
Wilson Spit Channel
Aquaculture
Whiting on edge of bank.
Bellarine Bank
Snapper.
BELLARINE
Portarlington Road
GRAVE YARD
Nov - Jan: whiting
Clifton Springs Jetty
Spoil Ground
CLIFTON SPRINGS
Scotchmans Road
Whitcombes Founds Road
PORT PHILLIP BAY
Jetty Road
Drysdale-St Leonards Road
DRYSDALE

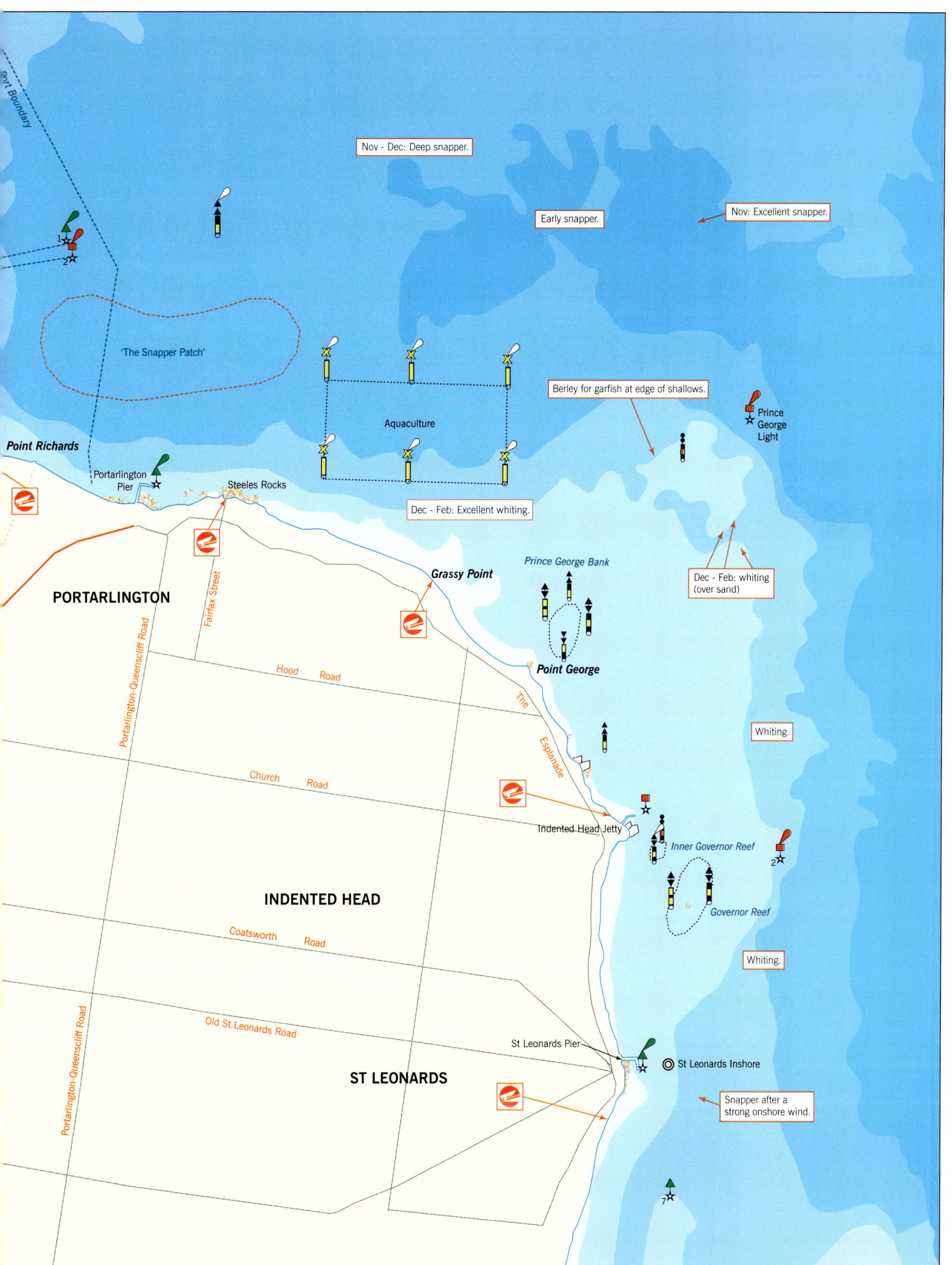
Port Boundary
Nov - Dec: Deep snapper.
Early snapper.
Nov: Excellent snapper.
1
2
'The Snapper Patch'
Aquaculture
Berley for garfish at edge of shallows.
Prince George Light
Point Richards
Portarlington Pier
Steeles Rocks
Dec - Feb: Excellent whiting.
Grassy Point
Prince George Bank
Dec - Feb: whiting (over sand)
PORTARLINGTON
Fairfax Street
Portarlington-Queenscliff Road
Point George
Hood Road
The Esplanade
Whiting.
Church Road
Indented Head Jetty
Inner Governor Reef
2
INDENTED HEAD
Governor Reef
Coatsworth Road
Whiting.
Old St.Leonards Road
Portarlington-Queenscliff Road
St Leonards Pier
St Leonards Inshore
ST LEONARDS
Snapper after a strong onshore wind.
7

CHAPTER 3
CORIO BAY
MAPS 4 & 5

Corio Bay, midway between Queenscliff and Werribee along the western shoreline of Port Phillip Bay, is relatively safe for boating. The most dangerous blow comes from the northwest, but even then, it is a simple matter to drive around the bay and fish the north or west shores.

Corio Bay inner and outer harbours are shaped like an hourglass, with a distended northwest corner. Moving clockwise, Corio Bay commences at Portarlington on the southern side, follows an easterly direction to Geelong, and finishes at Pt Wilson on the north side. In between are the outer and inner harbours, and a small estuary known as Limeburners Bay, aka, the Grammar School Lagoon.

OUTER HARBOUR: SOUTHERN SHORE

Portarlington

Portarlington is at the southeast extremity of Corio Bay Outer Harbour. The harbour complex is a major attraction. Built to provide shelter for commercial fishers it offers opportunity for land-based anglers. The harbour is L-shaped with the main pier running north to south, and at the end of the pier, a rock wall forming a breakwater runs west to east.

In 2012, Fisheries Victoria installed an artificial reef on the seaward side of the rock wall on the pier. The reefs runs almost the entire length of this wall and is located at about 70 metres off the wall at the ends, and comes in within 40 m at the centre.

Anglers tend to fish set areas. Those chasing squid seem to concentrate their efforts at the end of the pier, on the Geelong side. Anglers looking for mullet or garfish will be found fishing with float rigs in the sheltered harbour. For those wanting to catch snapper, salmon, gummy sharks and whiting, the rock wall is the preferred place to set up a rod.

One of the nice things about Portarlington pier is that during the warmer months the southerly sea breeze comes in from behind, making it a comfortable fishing platform on most evenings.

Inshore there is plenty of whiting grounds, especially close to the mussel farms. You are not allowed to fish in the farms, but you can fish near them. From December through to May you can expect to take reasonable numbers of whiting, along with garfish and red mullet.

The deeper water produces flathead, elephant and gummy sharks and snapper. Top snapper spots include Seal Rocks, about a kilometre or so east of the harbour, and the Steam Packet Channel to the northeast. Snapper run right along the channel edges so you never know where you are likely to find them in good numbers.

STEAM PACKET CHANNEL
S38 04 890
E144 37 448
Fishes best from late spring, and again in autumn.

Pt Richards

Situated between Clifton Springs and Portarlington, Pt Richards has a sheltered harbour and two-lane boat ramp. The turnoff to the boat ramp is clearly signposted on the Geelong-Portarlington Road. When leaving the ramp, boaters need to be aware of the shallow sandbanks immediately north of the ramp. The safe way to head out is to go west the Cardinal mark before turning north.

Mussel farms to the west of the boat ramp are popular with anglers chasing whiting and pinkies. It is illegal to fish within the boundaries of these farms, but you can fish close and berley works well. Whiting are well spread and it is a matter of fishing in less than 5 m of water where seagrass is interspersed with sand holes. It is worth noting that seagrass beds can change from year to year so each season can be different in terms of location.

Snapper run right along the channel edges so you never know where you are likely to find them in good numbers. The deeper water also produces flathead, elephant and gummy sharks. Most snapper anglers fish within a couple of hundred metres of the channel, some prefer to fish along the edges or alternatively in the old Steampacket Channel almost directly offshore. During spring and summer, most big snapper are caught on the north side of the channel; as autumn roles in, snapper fishing is often better on the south side of the channel.

Portarlington harbour is close and land based anglers are well catered for with a pier and breakwall. The main pier runs north south, and at the end there is a breakwater that runs west to east. Salmon often run along here in good numbers, mullet, garfish and trevally are caught in the harbour and squid at the end of the pier on the western side. At this time of year, the southerly sea breeze comes in from behind, making it a comfortable fishing platform.

A couple of kilometres east of the harbour is Seal Rocks, and after a strong blow this area can be a hotspot for snapper within a kilometre of shore. Close by is a single lane boat ramp suited to boats to about 4.5 m. If you motor northwest across the channel there is a large area of reef that runs all the way to Pt Wilson and takes in Arthur the Great. This is a top area for snapper, sharks and whiting when you are in less than 5 m of water.

On calm evenings, it is common to see the glow of flounder lights along this stretch of coast as there are many sand areas and these can attract flounder in good numbers. Flounder spearing isn't exactly sportfishing but flounder are a tasty fish and there is always a good chance of spearing flathead.

Clifton Springs

Clifton Springs is a sheltered harbour with a double boat ramp, mooring jetty and toilets. The facility is well signposted and to get there, take the Portarlington Road out of Geelong, turning left at Jetty Rd just before Drysdale. Most anglers use this ramp as a launching place to reach areas in Corio Bay outer harbour and western Port Phillip Bay that are a bit far to travel to from Corio Bay. Snapper and whiting are the most sought after species, but anglers also catch flathead, garfish, snook, gummy sharks, elephant fish and squid.

The southern shore, from the Springs through to Pt Richards to the east, is home to extensive mussel farms. You are not allowed to fish in the farms, but you can fish near them. The hundreds of ropes hanging down with clusters of mussels growing on them is a big attraction to the fish. Most snapper anglers fish along the channel edges. As you move away from the channel, the bottom is heavy reef that is hard on terminal tackle. To overcome this most anglers will anchor away from the channel and throw back towards it as the banks along the top of the channel offer easier terrain to fish. On a southerly anglers fish the south side of the channel, on the northerly they cross the channel and drop anchor to face the south.

One of the most popular areas is the bend that marks the junction of the Wilson Spit and Pt Richards Channels. Better known as the elbow, this area attracts a lot of boat traffic when the snapper are on the go. The mark is the former flashing channel marker, and local anglers will tell you this has been moved about 150m along the channel towards Portarlington.

Buoy No. 6 on the south side of the channel marks the western edge of the Wilson Spit bank. On the south side of the channel, the bank averages about 5 m, but drops to about 9 m before the Curlewis Bank, this runs out about 300 m from the shore. The average depth of the Curlewis Bank is 2 m–3 m, all the way back to Pt Henry.

For anglers who prefer to fish close to the ramp. The weed beds that are adjacent to the Clifton Springs harbour are consistent for flathead and squid. About a kilometre offshore is a 7 m drop off that will produce whiting, flathead and pinkies.

Curlewis Bank

The Curlewis Bank is well regarded for its whiting fishing during late summer and autumn. However, this vast bank of sand, seagrass and spoil ground also produces snapper, snook, squid and flathead. It is also popular with soft plastic lure anglers who catch pinkies and flathead over the spoil ground.

Close to shore, the bottom has a dense covering of seagrass, and where there are gaps in the grassbeds, whiting and flathead are caught, along with calamari squid. The area also produces good numbers of snook.

The grounds out from Hermsley Rd, about halfway between Pt Henry and Clifton Springs, are popular for whiting anglers.

Pt Henry

Pt Henry is a sand spit point on the southern shore of Corio Bay and marks the demarcation between the inner and outer harbours. It is distinctive in that there is a large aluminium smelter and a long pier used to unload raw alumina for the factory. The pier is officially unavailable to anglers although every now and again you spy an angler fishing from the pier, usually an employee of Alcoa it is said.

The best fishing here is from boats. Anglers are able to launch small boats on the eastern side of the sand spit. Take care to check the shell grit is firm before you drive on it. Launching and retrieving boats is generally best at high tide. On low tide, anglers with small boats sometimes unhook their trailers and take them to their boats, pulling boat and trailer from the water with a towrope.

During summer, anglers trolling garfish alongside the pier sometimes hook yellowtail kingfish to about 6 kg. Other species caught near the pier include salmon, silver trevally, trevalla, flathead and snapper. The grounds surrounding the pier are the most productive. On the northern side, seagrass beds run out to the Wilson Spit Channel and these produce whiting, garfish, flathead and snook. Many anglers fish along the edges of both sides of the Wilson Spit Channel for snapper. On the northern side of this channel are some productive whiting grounds in about 5 m of water.

Anglers fishing for snapper on the southern side of the shipping channel are often to be found anchored near the shipping turning basin out from the end of the pier. Alternatively, on the south east side of the structure towards the Curlewis Bank, there are seagrass beds and an old spoil ground. This is a favourite area for anglers working soft plastic lures for snapper, rock flathead and snook.

The shallow waters around Port Phillip Bay support an excellent population of calamari year round.

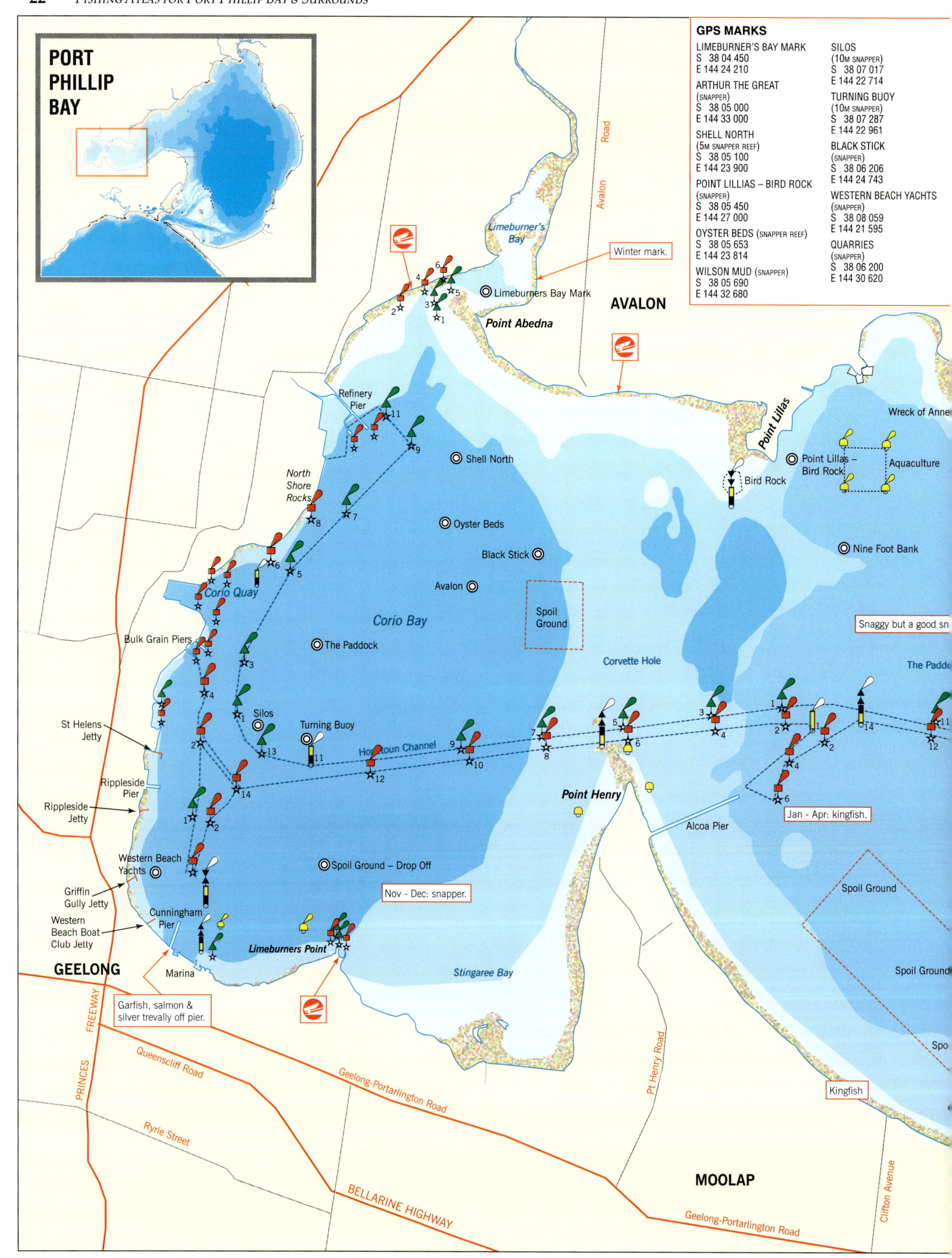
PORT PHILLIP BAY
GPS MARKS
LIMEBURNER'S BAY MARK
S 38 04 450
E 144 24 210
ARTHUR THE GREAT (SNAPPER)
S 38 05 000
E 144 33 000
SHELL NORTH (5M SNAPPER REEF)
S 38 05 100
E 144 23 900
POINT LILLIAS – BIRD ROCK (SNAPPER)
S 38 05 450
E 144 27 000
OYSTER BEDS (SNAPPER REEF)
S 38 05 653
E 144 23 814
WILSON MUD (SNAPPER)
S 38 05 690
E 144 32 680
SILOS (10M SNAPPER)
S 38 07 017
E 144 22 714
TURNING BUOY (10M SNAPPER)
S 38 07 287
E 144 22 961
BLACK STICK (SNAPPER)
S 38 06 206
E 144 24 743
WESTERN BEACH YACHTS (SNAPPER)
S 38 08 059
E 144 21 595
QUARRIES (SNAPPER)
S 38 06 200
E 144 30 620
Limeburner's Bay
Winter mark.
Limeburners Bay Mark
AVALON
Point Abedna
Avalon Road
Refinery Pier
Shell North
North Shore Rocks
Oyster Beds
Black Stick
Avalon
Corio Quay
Corio Bay
Spoil Ground
Bulk Grain Piers
The Paddock
Point Lillias
Point Lillias – Bird Rock
Bird Rock
Wreck of Anne
Aquaculture
Nine Foot Bank
Snaggy but a good sn
The Padd
Corvette Hole
St Helens Jetty
Silos
Turning Buoy
Hopetoun Channel
Point Henry
Alcoa Pier
Jan - Apr: kingfish.
Rippleside Pier
Rippleside Jetty
Western Beach Yachts
Spoil Ground – Drop Off
Nov - Dec: snapper.
Griffin Gully Jetty
Western Beach Boat Club Jetty
Cunningham Pier
Limeburners Point
Spoil Ground
Spoil Ground
Stingaree Bay
GEELONG
Marina
Garfish, salmon & silver trevally off pier.
PRINCES FREEWAY
Queenscliff Road
Geelong-Portarlington Road
Pt Henry Road
Spo
Kingfish
Ryrie Street
BELLARINE HIGHWAY
MOOLAP
Geelong-Portarlington Road
Clifton Avenue

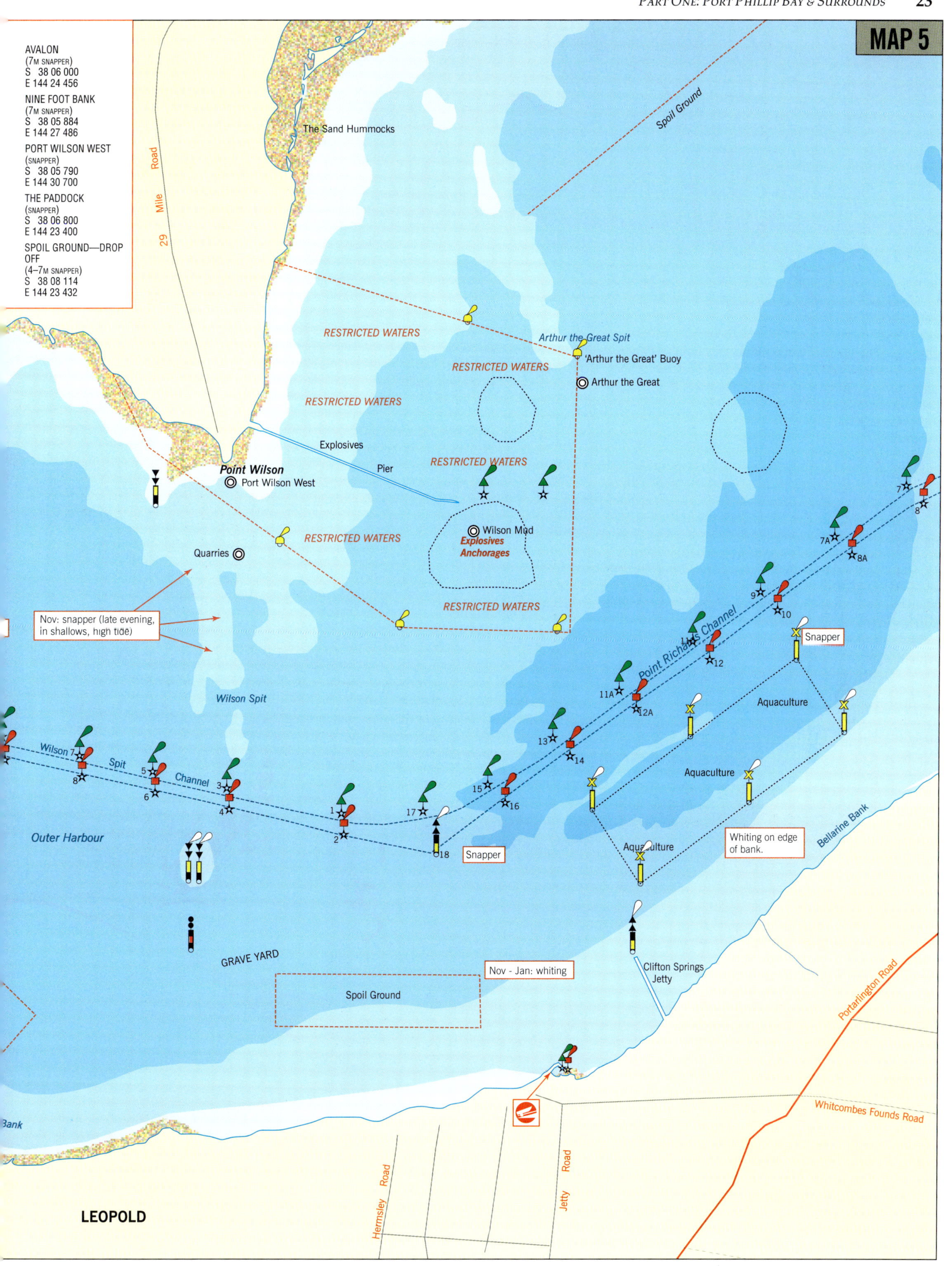
MAP 5
AVALON
(7M SNAPPER)
S 38 06 000
E 144 24 456
NINE FOOT BANK
(7M SNAPPER)
S 38 05 884
E 144 27 486
PORT WILSON WEST
(SNAPPER)
S 38 05 790
E 144 30 700
THE PADDOCK
(SNAPPER)
S 38 06 800
E 144 23 400
SPOIL GROUND—DROP OFF
(4–7M SNAPPER)
S 38 08 114
E 144 23 432
29 Mile Road
The Sand Hummocks
Spoil Ground
RESTRICTED WATERS
Arthur the Great Spit
'Arthur the Great' Buoy
Arthur the Great
Explosives Pier
Point Wilson
Port Wilson West
Wilson Mud
Explosives Anchorages
Quarries
Nov: snapper (late evening, in shallows, high tide)
Wilson Spit
Wilson Spit Channel
Point Richards Channel
Snapper
Aquaculture
Outer Harbour
Whiting on edge of bank.
Bellarine Bank
GRAVE YARD
Nov - Jan: whiting
Spoil Ground
Clifton Springs Jetty
Portarlington Road
Whitcombes Founds Road
Bank
Hermsley Road
Jetty Road
LEOPOLD

WESTERN SHORE

STINGRAY BAY

Stingray Bay on the southern shore is properly called Stingaree Bay, but many anglers simply refer to it as Limeburners, due to the boat harbour at Limeburners Pt. The boundary of the bay is roughly between the Limeburners Pt boat ramp complex and the sand spit at Pt Henry that abuts the main shipping channel. This bay produces a consistent variety of quality species.

Shore based anglers can do well off the rock walls catching snapper, luderick, garfish, whiting and flathead. For anglers with boats, whiting often run in good numbers, with the best results usually coming from the Spoil Ground, which is situated along the 5-metre line a couple of kilometres north east of the ramp. First and last light is the optimum time for the better whiting, particularly when this coincides with a tide change. During the day, pinkies can be a problem; the Spoil Ground also turns up some good flathead, mainly yanks but they can be to 2 kg. Snapper are a serious prize in these waters and the biggest snapper are caught inside an imaginary line that runs from the boat ramp across to the Pt Henry weather station. In other words, work inside the bay in the shallower areas for the big snapper. Fishing for snapper can be excellent, especially from about mid-autumn through the winter months when the stingrays have moved on. Daylight snapper are mainly pinkies, and many of these will be undersize. After sunset though, bigger snapper in the 3–6 kg brackets, come and go. The run of fish isn't as consistent as some anglers like but at least it is an opportunity to catch snapper through winter.

One of the quirks of this bay is the tidal flow. It doesn't seem to matter whether the tide is on the flood or the ebb; water movement is always east towards Pt Henry. The boat ramp consists of a double and a single ramp and will handle boats up to about 7 m with ease. There are pontoon jetties to tie your boat off, well-lit car parking and a wash down area. Unlike many Port Phillip Bay ramps, there is no launching fee and the fish cleaning facilities are a treat.

CUNNINGHAM PIER

Cunningham Pier is popular - it is privately owned and fishing hours are restricted, but at least you can drive your car on the pier and fish next to it. The seagrass beds along this shore produce solid catches of whiting.

In winter, boating anglers chasing snapper work along the western shore, from the entrance to Corio Quay, past St Helens, along Western Beach and between the Geelong Yacht Club marina and Cunningham pier. Boat ramps are located at St Helens and Limeburners Point. From spring through to autumn, snapper can be caught along the channel edges and in the "Paddock", on the east side of the shipping channel. When the snapper are in the bay, sometimes they need a trigger to start feeding. Two triggers that can bring the fish on are a strong blow from the east that stirs the water up, and Full or New Moon phases. The prime time to fish is generally an hour each side of a tide change.

One of the popular snapper spots for boaters is the Western Beach Bommie. This is a sunken yacht, with mast and sail intact.

WESTERN BEACH BOMMIE
S38 08 017
E144 21 709

Land based anglers don't have the mobility of boaters, but they still are able to catch snapper, and some other land based spots worth fishing include St Helens boat harbour rock wall, Griffin Gully jetty, Cunningham pier and Limeburners Point breakwalls on the southern shore. Cunningham pier is noted for its runs of trevalla, and most of the year has bream swimming between its pilings.

The western shore from St Helens through to the Cunningham pier can be very productive for big snapper from autumn through to spring. The ground between St Helens and the shipping channel and south to the former tugboat complex at Rippleside is highly regarded. Moreover, snapper can be caught among the Western Beach boat moorings, with whiting and trevally often in good numbers closer to shore.

From the Rippleside Pier going north, you pass a large industrial and waterfront area that includes an oil refinery and fertiliser factory complex.

The next fishable shore based water is North Shore rocks, just outside the entrance to Corio Quay. During winter, snapper that have remained in the bay tend to congregate along the western shore and these rocks are popular for that reason.

SILOS
S38 07 017
E144 22 714
Mud bottom, 10m of water out from the wheat silos and less than five minutes northeast of St Helens boat ramp. Can fish well during October and November.

Almost directly out from the Refinery Pier is a stretch of rough ground known as the Oyster Beds. This area is always worth a fish for snapper. Here is a mark:

OYSTER BEDS
S38. 05. 653
E144. 23. 814
Fishes best in October–December, and again from March to July.

LEFT: Pier fishing for snapper in season is very productive; just ensure you have a long net to aid in landing such a great catch.

INNER SHORE

Limeburners Bay

At the northern end of the bay is Limeburners Bay, one of the most famous waters in Port Phillip Bay. Overlooked by the Geelong Grammar School campus, this water is better known by most anglers as the Grammar School Lagoon. It isn't big water. Shaped like a figure eight with two small bays divided in part by a spit of sand, the Lagoon features a channel running in from Corio Bay at the western entrance, and is separated from the main bay by another sand spit, Pt Abeona. At the back of the Lagoon is Hovell Creek, which flows in past some mangroves and produces black bream.

Most anglers know the Lagoon for its legendary winter snapper fishing, however, this water produces a lot more than big winter snapper. It offers a diverse year round fishery with a mixed bag of species and is easily accessible for both boat and shore based angling. My most vivid memories of the Lagoon are based around 4.20 am. This was when the light in the grammar school clock tower went off, and was signal for regular anglers who fished the snapper here to change all baits in expectation of a fish at dawn.

The wonderful aspect of this water is that you never know what you are likely to hook. The channel edges can produce good catches of southern blue spotted (yank) flathead to 2.5 kg, and the same area is used by schools of salmon and mullet. Apart from the usual run of banjo sharks, stingrays and eagle rays, the lagoon can produce whiting, gummy sharks and even small mulloway. Contrary to popular legend, snapper have been caught in this water in every month of the year, not just the colder months.

Hovell Creek is highly regarded for its bream; these fish are also taken from the sand spit on the southern shore and most likely school around the boat moorings of the Lagoon Boat Club.

Tide and current are major factors influencing the movement of fish in and out of this water. The best time to fish it is when the high tide coincides with sunrise. Fish like snapper and mulloway move in on the flood tide to feed on the crabs, and leave on the ebb tide. If you catch a few fish when the tide is flooding, be sure and stay for a couple of hours of the run off tide. Flathead seem to be resident here most of the summer and autumn, and bream can be caught all year. The salmon and mullet are often best from about March through to October. Some years, schools of large salmon have taken up residence and anglers trolling along the channel edges, or casting from the beach using small silver wobblers have done well.

Avalon Beach

Following the inner harbour around from Limeburners Bay you pass Avalon Beach, little more than a collection of old huts. There is a boat ramp at the west end of Avalon Beach and the seagrass beds between the old channel and the shore are known for whiting and flounder. The old channel, which produces snapper particularly in spring, runs into the western end of the harbour, finishing in Corio Quay.

When targeting snapper in the Bay, you don't need to fish with heavy tackle.

OUTER HARBOUR: NORTHERN SHORE

Heading east from Avalon is Bird Rock and then further east is a Cardinal mark for the Aneora reef, named after a shipwreck. The reef rises to within a metre of the surface at high tide and parts of it are exposed on low tides. There is a significant drop off along sections of this reef and it produces good numbers of small snapper.

ANEORA
S38.05.505
E144.28.401

Farther east is an area known as the Nine Foot Bank. Regarded as a top snapper spot, the bank is located at:

NINE FOOT BANK
S38 05 884
E144 27 486

Weed, lice and flathead can be a problem, but the fishing can make it worth the effort. Fishes best from July through to October.

Bird Rock

Opposite Pt Henry on the northern side of the outer harbour. Anglers also fish here for whiting, garfish, flathead, gummy sharks and snook. Be careful not to venture too close to Bird Rock because, as the name suggests, it is a rocky point and shallows out for a fair way in parts. This rock used to be a popular land based option, with anglers fishing the eastern face where it fronts a small bay, casting out about 50 m into a channel that runs north-south along the eastern face.

POINT LILLIAS (BIRD ROCK)
S38. 05. 450
E144. 27 000
Produces snapper from August to April; the New Moon in October and November is often reliable.

The main shipping channel runs in on the southern side past Pt Henry, while the original, natural channel, passes Bird Rock.

Asha Day displays the fruits of fishing an early morning on the snapper.

Known as "The Old Channel", it produces snapper.

A sandbar that crosses between these channels divides the inner and outer harbours. Anglers fish along the edges of this sandbar for flathead and whiting. On the west or inner harbour side is a spoil ground, which fishes well for whiting and flathead in the autumn, and snapper in the spring.

POINT WILSON

Due north of Clifton Springs is Pt Wilson, distinguished by the long explosives pier. Boating restrictions apply and anglers need to stay 300 m away from the pier at all times. The grounds surrounding the pier produce snapper and King George whiting. East of the explosives pier is Arthur The Great, a popular snapper reef featuring a deep-water drop off. This reef fishes best for snapper from November through to March.

ARTHUR THE GREAT
S38. 05. 000
E144. 33. 000

The shallow grounds around Pt Wilson produce good numbers of whiting, sand and rock flathead, calamari squid and pinkies. The most productive water is from 3 m to 6 m.

The shoreline from Pt Wilson to Bird Rock, which makes up the north side of Corio Bay Outer Harbour, is rock strewn, so be careful going in too close to shore. A Cardinal marker between the Quarries and Pt Wilson, about a kilometre off shore, marks a boulder-strewn reef so stay well clear. About half way between Pt Wilson and Pt Lillias (aka Bird Rock) is a Quarry, and on the shoreline are the wrecks of a couple of barges.

If you motor west along the Wilson Spit Channel towards Geelong, you will come across the Wilson Spit Bank. Well regarded for its snapper fishing, the bank runs from the north shore of Corio Bay outer harbour to the southern shore near Clifton Springs, where it meets the Curlewis Bank. Buoy No. 5 on the north side and No. 6 on the south side of the channel mark the western edge of the bank; Buoys 3 and 4 mark the eastern edge.

On the west side, the bank drops into about 8 m of water, on the east side it is about 6m. The fishing along here includes all of the aforementioned species, and gummy sharks. Whiting are sought in 3–6 m of water, and snapper from about 5m out to the edge of the shipping channel. This applies all along this side of the bay.

QUARRIES
S38. 06. 200
E144. 30. 620
October to March, with October to January the best months.

POINT WILSON WEST
S38. 05. 790
E144. 30. 700
November to February the best times. Shallow ground, reef, and best at night.

WILSON MUD
S38. 05. 690
E144. 32. 680
Deep water, rougher the day the better the fishing can be. November to March the best times; often produces many pinkies.

Fresh bait is the key to success and garfish are readily available to catch, even while fishing for snapper.

CHAPTER 4
POINT WILSON TO POINT COOK
MAPS 6, 7 & 8

This stretch of Port Phillip Bay is a favoured area to fish though for a time the fishing had a lean patch. However, fishing like all things has cycles and a time, the area is back firing like the good old days.

The make-up of the bottom here is varied. The majority is seagrass and weed areas which make an ideal environment or whiting, flathead, trevally, garfish and a host of other species like the much maligned leatherjacket. It also is home to huge numbers of southern calamari.

There are also patches of heavy reef which, although at times posing a boating hazard, offer some great fishing. The main reef areas are terrific fishing spots on their day. The best reef areas are north-east of the RAAF Pier at Point Cook, Long Reef at Kirk Point and Arthur the Great Spit at Point Wilson.

The use of berley in any area is essential to consistent good results. Of course the rule with berley is that you want to tempt the fish and not feed them, so the old saying of a little often applies here. The idea of berley is to get the fish into a feeding frenzy. An added advantage when using berley consistently is that a range of fish species can end up attracted to the fishing area.

A favoured fish in this area is the flathead that many anglers know as 'Yanks'. They are in fact long-nose flathead, the solid ones with the blue spots, and they are one of the best eating fish in the bay. The best time for flatties here is early in winter around June and July.

However it is the big two (in profile that is) which anglers come to this area for: snapper and the King George whiting.

Concern for this area is the amount of damage that professional netters do to the sea bed. It is believed that it is unfair that anglers are constrained, and rightly so, by bag limits, yet licensed commercial netters can indiscriminately drag nets over the delicate weed bottom and take everything in their path.

WHERE TO FISH – BOAT FISHING

Using GPS (Global Positioning System), an electronic aid to navigation, there is only a general description of ground rather than pin-pointing the spot. However, a few special spots have been listed which, if you fish them, can be productive.

Given the fact that angling attention has increased tenfold in places over the years, there is never any doubt about which areas are producing. Just look for the groups of boats and that is usually where some action is happening. Some species like whiting often come on the bite better with the accumulation of craft. However, you should respect the space of anglers who are already on the mark.

EXPLOSIVES PIER

The public is prohibited from accessing this pier, however the ground either side of the pier is very good whiting and small snapper territory.

On the Melbourne side of the structure you will see areas of broken ground when the water is clear. These are generally weed and sand areas, and this ground continues right out almost to the end of the pier.

At certain times of the year, very small wrasse and strangers (also known as 'slimies') swarm here. Harder baits like squid or bass yabbies will keep them at bay for a while, and when small snapper or large flathead move in, the pests will move away. Often a move of only a few metres or casting slightly away from the boat can locate fish.

ARTHUR THE GREAT

This area follows a north-south line from the shore near the Control Tower at Avalon airfield.

Just recently some excellent whiting and large flathead have been found right on top of the spit. There is also a very steep drop-off either side of the spit that creates superb cover for 'pinky' snapper. Snapper have been caught here from 0.5 to 2 kg in the middle of the day. The essential conditions for this fishing are either overcast conditions or murky water following a heavy onshore blow. Of course the other 'hot' times are first and last light.

You should look at a Marine Chart of this area, or do some sounding with your depth sounder to get a feel for the drop-offs—essential to success here.

LONG REEF

This is a very popular area north-east of the boat ramp at Kirks. Caution must be used at very low tides—the bottom is littered with big reefy areas which can become quite a hazard.

Notwithstanding this, there are some excellent whiting patches here. Trevally has also been caught along with large flathead and small snapper on the same ground when using berley. Once again first light is an excellent time to fish; also the change of tide in the late afternoon can be very productive.

The south cardinal marker will signify the start of the reef and there is good fishing between here and Wedge Point. Also fair-size snook (sometimes incorrectly called pike) have been taken by trolling Rapala lures close to the reef. At times, the birds will indicate schools of salmon and these fish can give excellent sport either trolling, or casting lures into the school.

WEDGE POINT TO THE STICK

This is a very popular shallow water fishery that gets plenty of traffic from late November to Easter every season. The main target is the King George whiting, as the ground here is superb and almost perfect for whiting. There have also been thousands of garfish sighted on this ground.

Good conditions here are light south-easterlies and the first day of a northerly.

Best catches are made when you can see the bottom and therefore it best to cast well away from the boat and fish a longer leader on a paternoster rig than usual.

There is the slightest run in the tidal flow here so if a certain area is producing, fish two anchors, fore and aft as this will help keep you on the spot. Those anglers familiar with the bridle system for anchoring will find it useful here. One downside of this shallow water fishing is that running outboard motors can 'spook' the fish and put them off the bite or scare them away. When calling other boats in, or moving into the area yourself, bear this in mind and keep noise to a minimum. The introduction of 4 stroke motors has halved this problem.

WERRIBEE SOUTH

The area off the mouth of the Werribee River is very productive, however be aware that there are speed restrictions and other boating regulations that apply. A good working knowledge of the regulations will ensure you boat with safety.

There are many square kilometres of productive ground out from here. However this doesn't mean you catch fish all the time. You must locate the fish and because most of the time the water is over 4 m in depth and you cannot see the bottom, much of the preparation is trial and error. From my experience small moves of some 30 m can make a difference. The weed here is quite clumpy and a slight change in area can set you on a good sandy patch. When a patch of fish is found, take a shore mark or set the spot on your GPS.

Excellent catches of King George whiting, flathead, garfish and at times trevally abound in this area. There is really good fishing when the wind is in the east here. Many times there have been excellent catches in the dirty water no more than 200 metres from shore. So much for the east wind theory!

Late autumn or early winter is also a good time to drift for flathead and squid. When a good drift is found, either motor up and go over it again, or drop the anchor and berley straight away.

By no means are the GPS coordinates below meant to mark the magic spot. They are merely a guide to the grounds which have proven productive.

The area close in can be found at:

S - 38 00 01 26
E - 144 41 54 75.

The deeper area is:

S - 38 01 32 21
E - 144 41 53 58

SNAPPER GROUNDS

Many readers will recognise the term rubble. This is the ground preferred for snapper. Straight out from the Werribee River mouth about 6 kilometres from shore, there is plenty of ground that is 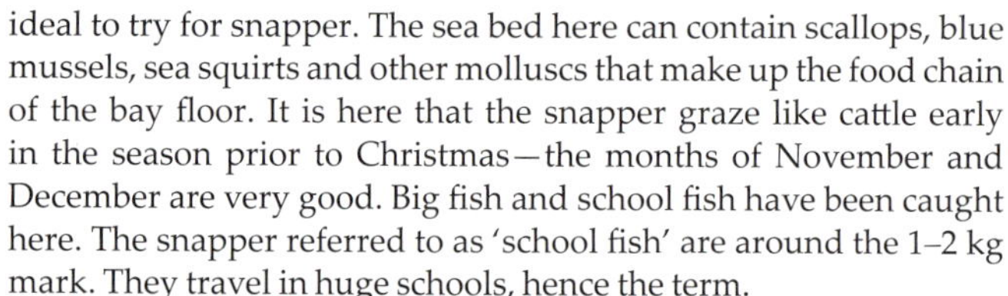ideal to try for snapper. The sea bed here can contain scallops, blue mussels, sea squirts and other molluscs that make up the food chain of the bay floor. It is here that the snapper graze like cattle early in the season prior to Christmas—the months of November and December are very good. Big fish and school fish have been caught here. The snapper referred to as 'school fish' are around the 1–2 kg mark. They travel in huge schools, hence the term.

But primarily anglers fish here for big snapper. It is among the very best areas in the bay for large snapper between November and December each season. Fine gummy sharks have also been taken here at times. Best conditions are a moderating southerly or immediately after a south-westerly blow. Small flathead can be a nuisance at times and constant checking of baits like pilchards is a must. There has been considerable success here on flathead fillets and whole garfish. Of late harder baits like couta and whiting heads have been successful for many anglers.

On many occasions in the early 1970's, it was found difficult to keep the hooked snapper away from the packs of bronze whaler sharks. In the mid 1980's, for some reason the lack of sharks coincided with a downturn in the fishery. It is pleasing to note that packs of bronze whalers are once more entering the bay. It has been found that packs of small sharks, bronze whalers and school sharks are never far away from schools of snapper.

There is not a GPS co-ordinate here as the mark is easily located and has produced year in year out. This mark can be picked up when travelling east from the Werribee River mouth. After travelling about 3.5 km, look left in the direction of the CBD to the Point Cook trees. The cracking tower at Altona Refinery (the one with the fire on top) cuts the right hand edge of the trees just before they hit the point. Looking back to the west, the You Yangs will be visible with three humps. The extreme right hand hump is known as `The Pimple'. Place the left hand side on the pine plantation to the left of the river mouth, on The Pimple. The pine plantation will appear as an oblong hedge when out in the bay.

DUNCANS

This area is about 2 km offshore from Duncans Road and is an underrated area for whiting, gummy sharks and snapper. Some very large flathead have been taken here at anchor whilst fishing for snapper in heavy seas.

There are also odd patches of heavy reef which obviously attract snapper and there are some very nice garfish at times, especially on a northerly.

The coordinates are:

S - 37 58 38 00
E - 144 42 37 14

POINT COOK AIRFIELD AND JETTY

The pier is in disrepair and is not recommended. However the area around the pier takes in some terrific ground. It appears that the schools of small snapper are making a return and the last couple of whiting seasons have been promising. Once again this area is very general. Constant moving, berleying and paying attention to detail with baits and where you cast, all add up to a successful day on the water.

Towards Point Cook there is

LEFT: Fishing the shallow reefs with soft plastics is a popular affair throughout the year on pinkie snapper.

In calm conditions, snapper fishing can be tough. Stick with it and work hard to be rewarded.

some extremely heavy ground. A professional netter used to live at Campbell's Cove shacks in the late 60's and early 70's. He made a good living from long-lining and netting this area and he regularly took good catches of gummy sharks and yellowtail kingfish.

A very good mark here comes from a legend in the area, Mr Ted Oliver, and is:

S - 37 57 32 63
E - 144 48 25 63

CUNNINGHAMS

This is one of the favourite marks in the bay, not so much for its production of any one species, but for its ability to produce a wide variety of fish on any given day. Good conditions are a southerly or light northerly, while late afternoon and evening seem to be a very good time to fish.

Early in the season, some big snapper move through this area and local anglers always nail a few good ones. There have been some extraordinary hauls from here in October in the dark of the night. When the whiting turn up, the smaller snapper move in also and it pays to carry a measure as some of both species can struggle to make the size limit.

Some quality whiting has been caught here in June, but those that fish the area regularly will know this is rare. It appears that when the water temperature falls dramatically the fish go off the bite.

The mark is quite simple. Behind the end of the RAAF Pier to the left, there is a double clump of cypress trees about a kilometre back. Line this up, then look north and place the Altona cracking tower in the middle of the Point Cook trees.

Caution for Small Boats

Small boat operators should be aware of the very heavy, sometimes exposed reef, north of the RAAF Pier. Extreme caution is required when navigating this area, especially when the water is discoloured. It is strongly suggested that you purchase a map of the area and have a thorough working knowledge of this reef. If you have time, inspection at low water can give you a very good idea of the dangers here. That said it is also a haven for fish.

BOAT RAMPS

Kirk Point: There is a concrete boat ramp at Kirk Point. It is found at the end of Beach Road and is reached by turning down 29 Mile Road off the Geelong Freeway. Waders are often an advantage here as the onshore winds from the south and east make launching a nightmare.

Beacon Point: Smaller craft can be launched off the shell shore near Beacon Point. However, as this is not a public road, a permit from Melbourne Water is required to access this area (see the Werribee River section of this book for details).

Although the ramp at the Werribee River mouth is some distance away, it is preferrable in good weather to use these facilities. Unfortunately over the past few years it has become a risk to leave cars and trailers parked in the Kirk Point area. It is disappointing, but on days when there is not much traffic about it can become a real problem.

SHORE BASED FISHING

Quite a few anglers line the shore between Duncan's Road and the first lot of huts at Campbell's Cove. They generally chase the large flathead that move inshore during summer. In the dark of the night after Christmas some fish have topped 3 kg on the scales. A whole pilchard or squid pieces will do the trick. Most big flathead are taken either at night or after a strong onshore blow from the south-east.

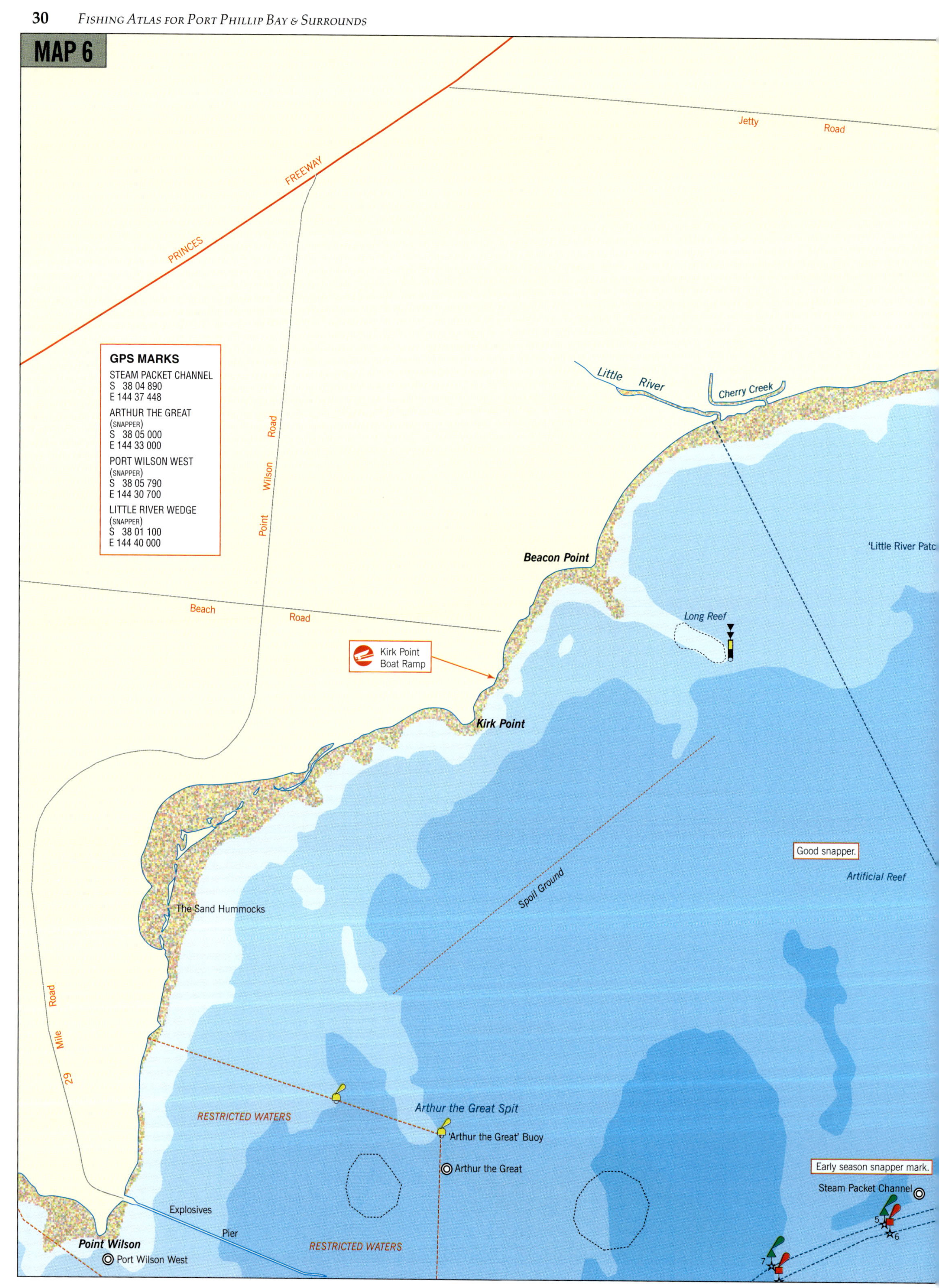
MAP 6
GPS MARKS
STEAM PACKET CHANNEL
S 38 04 890
E 144 37 448
ARTHUR THE GREAT
(SNAPPER)
S 38 05 000
E 144 33 000
PORT WILSON WEST
(SNAPPER)
S 38 05 790
E 144 30 700
LITTLE RIVER WEDGE
(SNAPPER)
S 38 01 100
E 144 40 000
PRINCES FREEWAY
Jetty Road
Point Wilson Road
Beach Road
29 Mile Road
Little River
Cherry Creek
Beacon Point
'Little River Patc
Long Reef
Kirk Point Boat Ramp
Kirk Point
Good snapper.
Artificial Reef
Spoil Ground
The Sand Hummocks
Arthur the Great Spit
RESTRICTED WATERS
'Arthur the Great' Buoy
Arthur the Great
Early season snapper mark.
Steam Packet Channel
Explosives Pier
Point Wilson
Port Wilson West
RESTRICTED WATERS

PORT
PHILLIP
BAY
COCOROC
Werribee River
Diggers Road
O'Connors Road
Beach Road
Salmon & mulloway
Mulloway
Werribee River Boat Ramp
Good flathead.
'Werribee Patch'
Evening snapper on high tide (Nov - Dec).
Wedge Point
Good snapper (Nov)
'The Pimple'
Wedge Spit
Calamari over broken ground.
Little River Wedge
Excellent snapper (Nov)
'Channel Rubbly'
Aquaculture
Nov - Dec: Deep snapper.
Entrance Beacon
Early snapper.
Nov: Excellent snapper.
'The Snapper Patch'

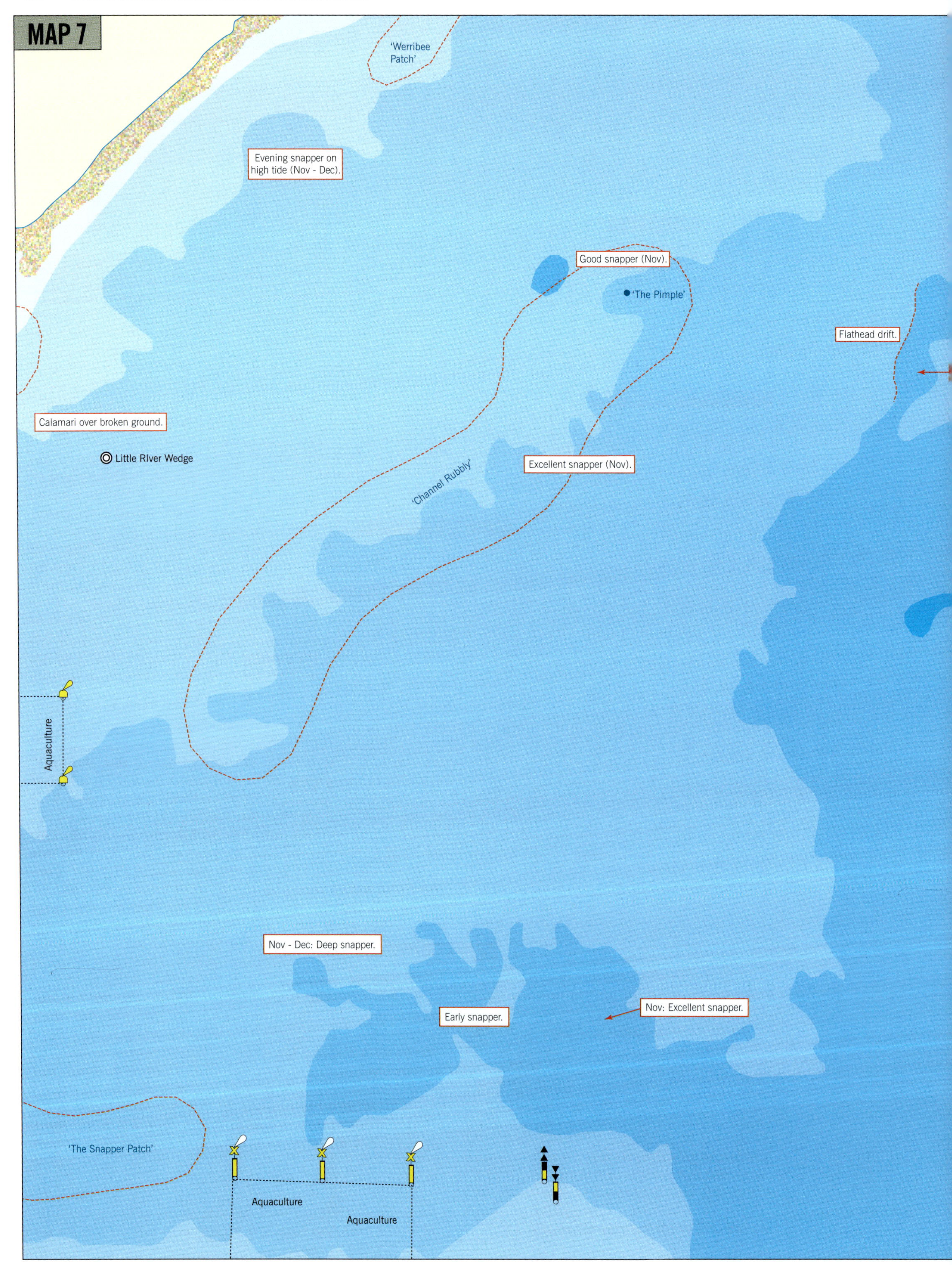
MAP 7
'Werribee Patch'
Evening snapper on high tide (Nov - Dec).
Good snapper (Nov).
'The Pimple'
Flathead drift.
Calamari over broken ground.
Little River Wedge
'Channel Rubbly'
Excellent snapper (Nov).
Aquaculture
Nov - Dec: Deep snapper.
Early snapper.
Nov: Excellent snapper.
'The Snapper Patch'
Aquaculture
Aquaculture

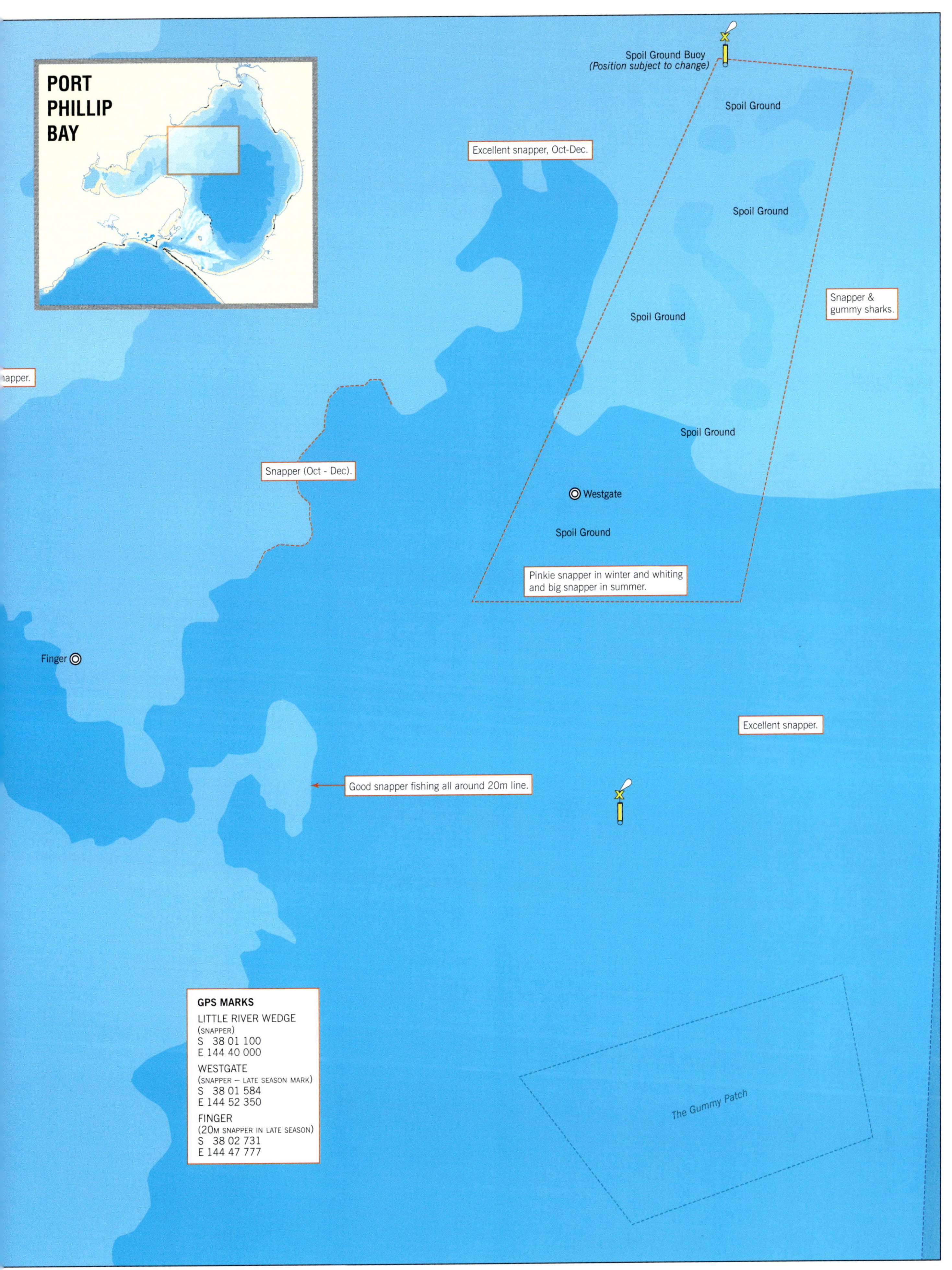
PORT PHILLIP BAY
Spoil Ground Buoy
(Position subject to change)
Spoil Ground
Excellent snapper, Oct-Dec.
Spoil Ground
Snapper & gummy sharks.
Spoil Ground
Spoil Ground
Snapper (Oct - Dec).
Westgate
Spoil Ground
Pinkie snapper in winter and whiting and big snapper in summer.
Finger
Excellent snapper.
Good snapper fishing all around 20m line.
The Gummy Patch
GPS MARKS
LITTLE RIVER WEDGE
(SNAPPER)
S 38 01 100
E 144 40 000
WESTGATE
(SNAPPER – LATE SEASON MARK)
S 38 01 584
E 144 52 350
FINGER
(20M SNAPPER IN LATE SEASON)
S 38 02 731
E 144 47 777

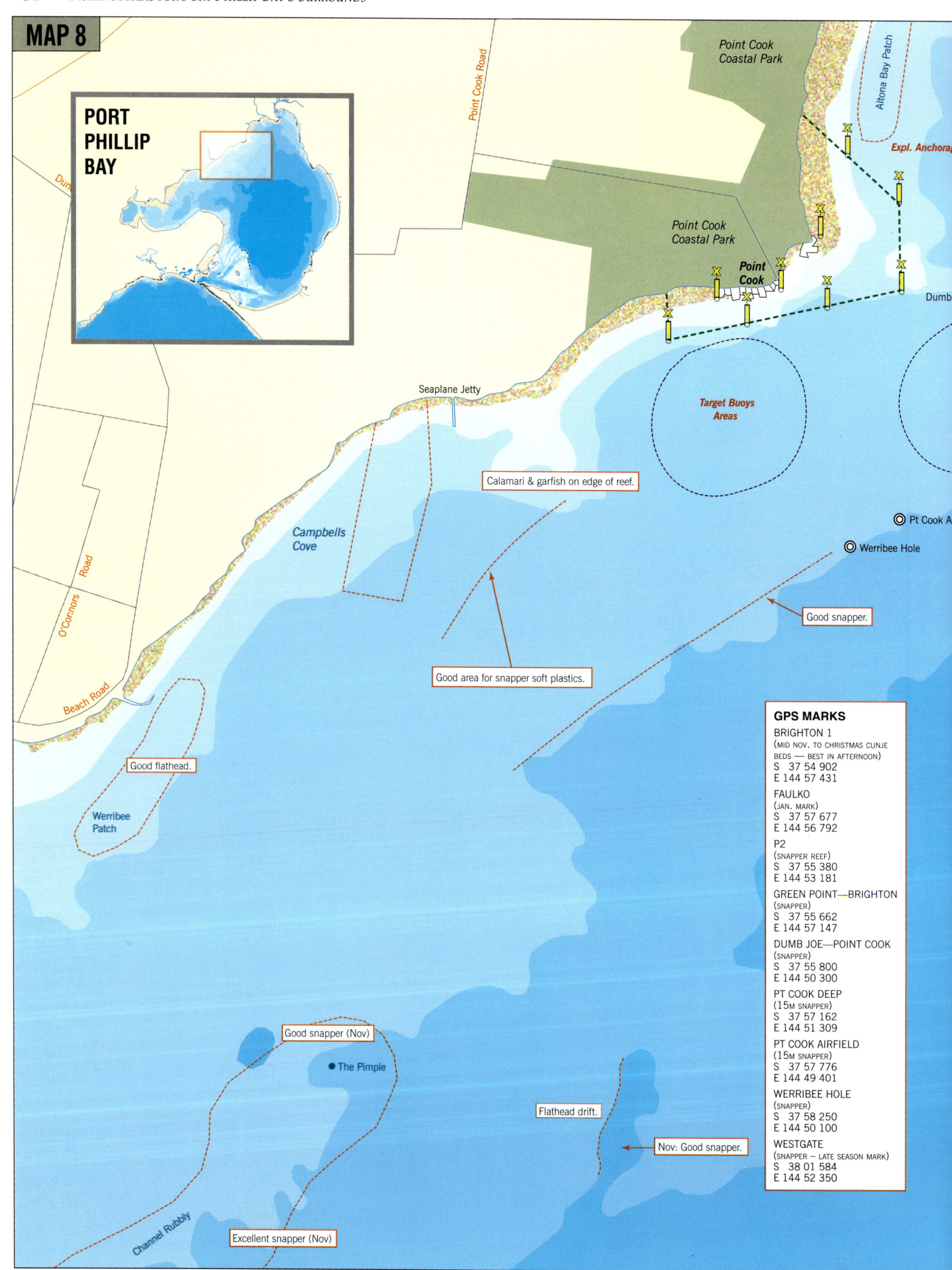

GPS MARKS

BRIGHTON 1
(MID NOV. TO CHRISTMAS CUNJE BEDS — BEST IN AFTERNOON)
S 37 54 902
E 144 57 431

FAULKO
(JAN. MARK)
S 37 57 677
E 144 56 792

P2
(SNAPPER REEF)
S 37 55 380
E 144 53 181

GREEN POINT—BRIGHTON
(SNAPPER)
S 37 55 662
E 144 57 147

DUMB JOE—POINT COOK
(SNAPPER)
S 37 55 800
E 144 50 300

PT COOK DEEP
(15M SNAPPER)
S 37 57 162
E 144 51 309

PT COOK AIRFIELD
(15M SNAPPER)
S 37 57 776
E 144 49 401

WERRIBEE HOLE
(SNAPPER)
S 37 58 250
E 144 50 100

WESTGATE
(SNAPPER – LATE SEASON MARK)
S 38 01 584
E 144 52 350

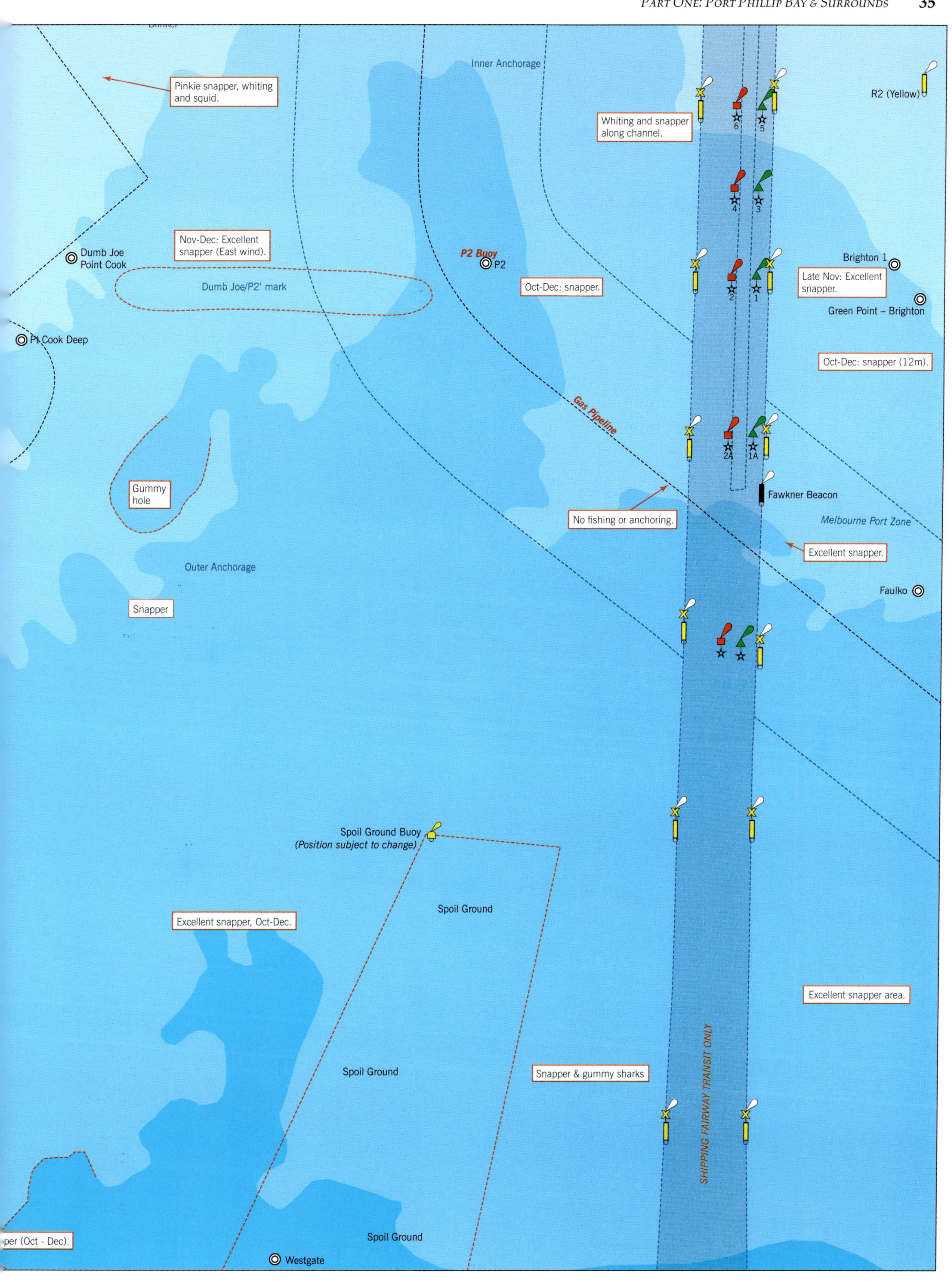
Inner Anchorage
Pinkie snapper, whiting and squid.
Whiting and snapper along channel.
R2 (Yellow)
Nov-Dec: Excellent snapper (East wind).
Dumb Joe Point Cook
Dumb Joe/P2' mark
P2 Buoy
P2
Oct-Dec: snapper.
Brighton 1
Late Nov: Excellent snapper.
Green Point – Brighton
Pt Cook Deep
Oct-Dec: snapper (12m).
Gas Pipeline
Gummy hole
Fawkner Beacon
No fishing or anchoring.
Melbourne Port Zone
Excellent snapper.
Outer Anchorage
Faulko
Snapper
Spoil Ground Buoy
(Position subject to change)
Spoil Ground
Excellent snapper, Oct-Dec.
Excellent snapper area.
Spoil Ground
Snapper & gummy sharks
SHIPPING FAIRWAY TRANSIT ONLY
per (Oct - Dec).
Spoil Ground
Westgate

CHAPTER 5

POINT COOK TO WILLIAMSTOWN

MAP 9

This stretch of the bay is very popular with small craft operators who work the area hard during the season for King George whiting, snapper and squid. Gars swarm here in the warmer months and other species like leatherjackets, flounder, flathead and red mullet are prevalent.

The seabed between Point Cook and 'Willy' is a mixture of sand, weed, reef and rubble. Added to this are extensive scallop beds that are perfect areas for big snapper. Is it any wonder with such a good combination of sea floor that this is one of the most popular and productive areas in the bay?

This area has always productive, especially fishing in close on the broken ground of weed and sand. There has been some wonderful fishing here on light northerlies. Also, the strong south-westerlies that blow in November and December do not generate big seas in the shelter of 'The Cook' as they do elsewhere.

The area can be a hit or miss affair when the big snapper first enter the bay in October. However if you happen to hit the jackpot on a night they are 'on', then it can highlight just what a marvellous resource is here close to Melbourne. Peak times for this area are Melbourne Cup day to Easter. Winter fishing at times can be fruitful with calamari squid, large flathead and at times, huge schools of Australian salmon.

The area is also renowned for its pinky snapper run in the warmer months. In recent seasons this area has been very busy on the reefs with rods going off in all directions.

Now, on to sharks and how people seem petrified of them. If the small bronze whalers are following the schools of snapper, you know the snapper are going to be on the job. Sharks mean plenty of food and in this case plenty of snapper.

Anglers should note that in the summer months the sea breezes from the south-east can create some very nasty seas in this part of the bay.

WHERE TO FISH – BOAT FISHING

Anglers should be aware of the 290 hectare Point Cooke Marine Sanctuary, which extends offshore from the Point Cook Coastal Park. No fishing is permitted within the sanctuary, which is marked by shore markers and in-water navigation marks. Contact Parks Victoria for exact details of sanctuary boundaries

DUMB JOE

This used to be a buoy but has since been replaced by a cardinal marker on top of a pylon. It signifies shallow ground west of the pile. Basically the drop-off is outside the marker and the shallow reef area is inside towards the shore.

Those anglers that enjoy catching leatherjackets will have a ball here. The heavy reef, kelp and weed areas are home to thousands of 'leatheries', and if you fish over the heavy ground, you get more fish. If looking for whiting and you can see the bottom, it is best to anchor on the heavy dark area and throw into the light patches which will be sand and shell.

The area between the pylon and Point Cook (but outside the sanctuary) is prime whiting ground. It has been found that it best to fish in 2 to 3 m of water and throw away from the boat using very little weight here on an extended paternoster rig.

It is in these shallow areas when the fish are finicky, that the sloppy action of a slow tapered rod comes into its own. Everywhere you will see anglers, young and old, pulling like billyo when they get a nibble. It is best to let the fish take the bait and when you feel that solid pull, just lift the rod.

When targeting snapper, fan your baits out to increase your chance at success.

Passing ships are a catalyst for success. Seasoned anglers know that an approaching ship can cause snapper in the area to come on the bite for a brief period.

P2 Buoy

This buoy is located about 6 km off Altona. It marks the course of the underwater gas pipeline and the law prevents anchoring within 150 m of the line. The ground is general here and is ideal for grazing snapper. It's not that it is such a good spot, it just gives the anglers a starting point when fishing. Usually when word gets out about the fish being `on' at P2, it is like Bourke Street. Large snapper to 8 kg and averaging 2.5 kg are the usual run of fish here. It is also a good area for some nice flathead. Berley up around the boat while snapper fishing and you can catch a good feed. Flathead fillets make excellent bait as well. In summer, good quality gars are taken here.

Rifle Range

This area is off what used to be the Williamstown Rifle Range but this has since become a residential area. The area has prolific reef, weed and shell and therefore attracts whiting and snapper. It has been found that the weed here is full of butterfly shell, red-legged shrimps, small crabs and polychaete worms. This is surely a sign of a fishy area.

December to April is prime time but during many winters, there are resident schools of small snapper to be caught. As with many areas within the bay, the boats will soon let you know where the fish are biting. The days of marks are numbered, which seems a pity.

Best evenings are with the breeze in the south. You can catch both whiting and pinkys on the same mark. Berley will improve your chances and the pellet variety holds well amongst the reef. A few ling have been taken in the area and it is still the most consistent place in the bay for dusky morwong (butterfish).

BOAT RAMPS

Unfortunately this area is not well serviced with ramps. The closest are at Altona or Werribee but it is quite a run to the best spots. Nevertheless, seasoned anglers know it can be worth the effort.

Werribee River: An excellent ramp in all weather condition, concrete multi ramp with plenty of parking.

Altona: Another good concrete multi lane ramp that is protected in most winds with excellent parking

SHORE BASED FISHING

Altona Pier

This is quite a good pier for garfish in the summer. Northerlies or light westerlies are best here. A light bran berley will attract the gars to within casting distance. Yellow-eye mullet are also plentiful with sandworms the best bait.

On a recent trip to the pier in April, the squid were on the job and apparently the best time is late afternoon. In March, some monster flathead are also taken from the pier—the big breeding females come close to shore at this time of the year. Land-Based fishing to the right of the pier is also very productive for flathead in September through to December. The bottom is sand with deep divots and the flathead hunt for minnows on the high tide. Wading out and flicking soft plastics is a productive method.

Sandworms can be pumped along the foreshore here and Pier Street is a very good area. For those that require only a few bass yabbies for bream fishing at Werribee, the Williamstown piers or the Yarra, there are some nice yabbies to be pumped near the Altona Pier on the banks at low tide. Locate the hole of the yabby and place the bait pump over the top, then simply lift the handle and place the contents of the pump in a bait sieve or on the sand. Shrimps, which are also good bream bait, can be collected by running a bait scoop net amongst the weed along the shore between the pier and the boat ramp.

As with any fishing or bait gathering, be well aware of what the laws are in relation to gathering and possessing bait—consult your Victorian Recreational Fishing Guide for details.

MAP 9
GPS MARKS
BRIGHTON 1
(MID NOV. TO CHRISTMAS CUNJE BEDS — BEST IN AFTERNOON)
S 37 54 902
E 144 57 431
BRIGHTON 2
(SIMILAR AREA BRIGHTON 1 BUT CLOSER IN)
S37 54 556
E 144 57 775
ALTONA REEF
(SNAPPER)
S 37 52 761
E 144 51 515
DEAD MANS—WILLIAMSTOWN
(SNAPPER)
S 37 53 092
E 144 52 319
THE STICK
(REEF DEPTH 6–8 M NEAR ALTONA)
S 37 53 100
E 144 51 300
FOOTY GROUND—WILLIAMSTOWN
(9 M SNAPPER REEF)
S 37 53 284
E 144 53 960
OUTER FOOTY GROUND
(12–13 M SNAPPER)
S 37 53 785
E 144 53 904
P2
(SNAPPER REEF)
S 37 55 380
E 144 53 181
GREEN POINT—BRIGHTON
(SNAPPER)
S 37 55 662
E 144 57 147
DUMB JOE—POINT COOK
(SNAPPER)
S 37 55 800
E 144 50 300
PT COOK DEEP
(15M SNAPPER)
S 37 57 162
E 144 51 309
WEST GATE FREEWAY
PRINCES FREEWAY
Kororoit Creek
Millers Road
NEWPOR
Kororoit Creek Road
Maidstone Street
Altona Harbour
ALTONA
Altona Pier
Queen Street
Calamari
Flathead in shallows, calamari over weed.
Altona Reef
Wreck of Kakariki
Altona Reef
Year round calamari.
The Stick
Dead Ma
Williamst
Point Cook Road
Cheetham Wetlands
Altona Bay
P3 Buoy
An excellent area to target King George whiting and flathead.
'Altona Bay Patch'
'Blinker'
Pinkie snapper, whiting and squid.
Expl. Anchorage
Point Cook Coastal Park
Point Cook
Point Cook Marine Sanctuary
Dumb Joe Buoy
Dumb Joe – Point Cook
Nov–Dec: Excellent snapper (East wind).
'Dumb Joe/P2' mark
Pt Cook Deep
A good area for snapper before Christmas.
Target Buoys Areas
Expl. Anchorage
F Jetty

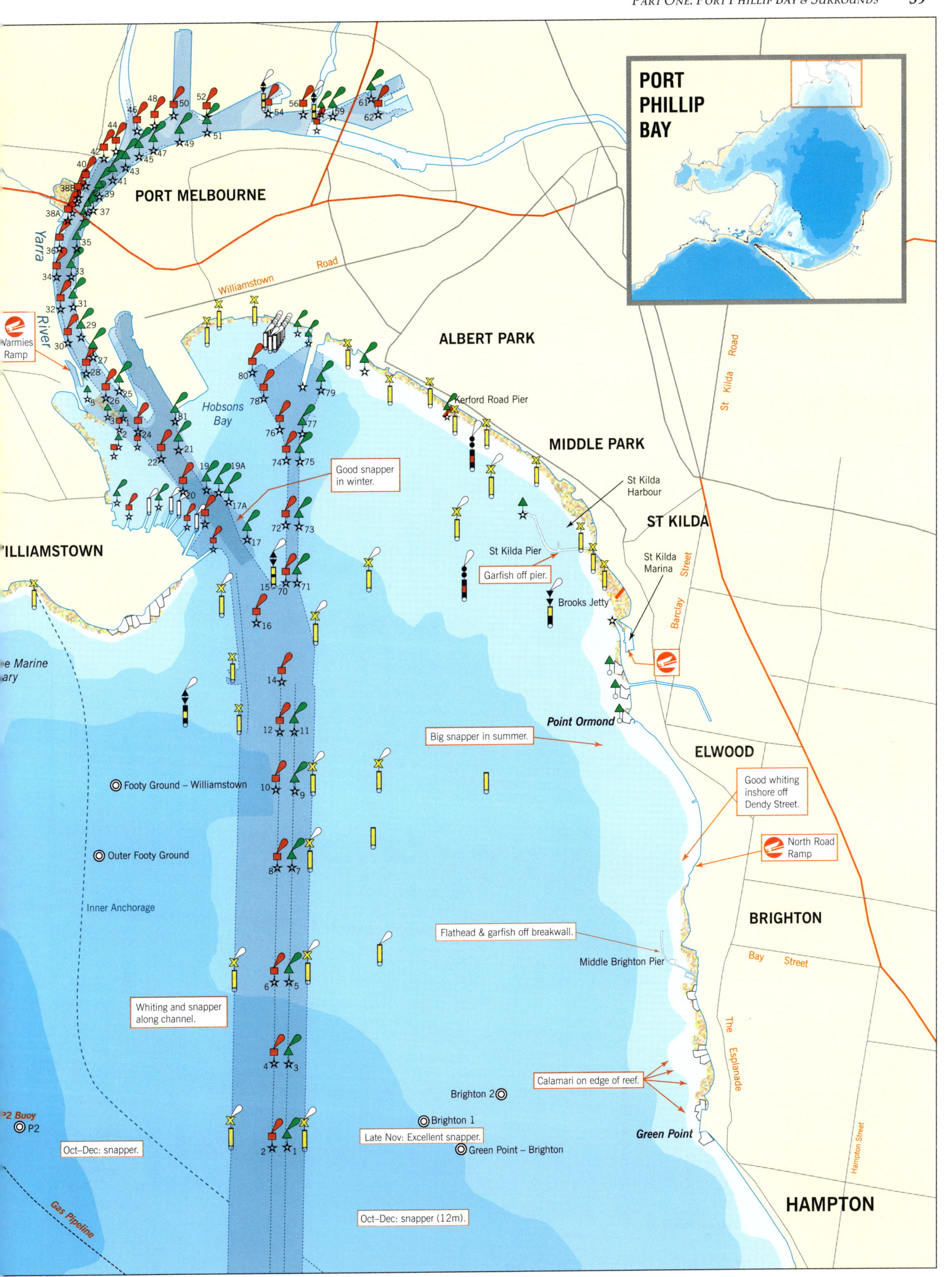
PORT PHILLIP BAY
PORT MELBOURNE
Yarra River
Williamstown Road
ALBERT PARK
MIDDLE PARK
Hobsons Bay
Kerford Road Pier
Good snapper in winter.
St Kilda Harbour
ST KILDA
St Kilda Pier
Garfish off pier.
St Kilda Marina
Brooks Jetty
Barclay Street
St Kilda Road
Point Ormond
Big snapper in summer.
ELWOOD
Good whiting inshore off Dendy Street.
North Road Ramp
Footy Ground – Williamstown
Outer Footy Ground
Inner Anchorage
BRIGHTON
Flathead & garfish off breakwall.
Middle Brighton Pier
Bay Street
The Esplanade
Whiting and snapper along channel.
Calamari on edge of reef.
Brighton 2
Brighton 1
Late Nov: Excellent snapper.
Green Point – Brighton
Green Point
Oct–Dec: snapper.
Gas Pipeline
Oct–Dec: snapper (12m).
Hampton Street
HAMPTON
Ramp

CHAPTER 6
WILLIAMSTOWN TO SANDRINGHAM
MAP 9

Out from Brighton nearing where the cargo ships enter the Yarra River is a prime location for big snapper throughout the season.

This section at the top of the bay takes in the Williamstown piers and harbour areas, the Port of Melbourne, Albert Park, St.Kilda, Elwood, Brighton and Sandringham. It is well serviced with launching ramps at Newport Power Station (known as the Hotties or Warmies), St.Kilda Marina and North Road boat ramp.

The fishing throughout this area can be outstanding, although it really pays to make sure you know your navigation rules and regulations. This is a busy port area and anchoring in the marked shipping lanes, or not adhering to speed limits, can see you cop a certain fine.

The boat ramps mentioned give great access to all of the top of the bay and best of all it doesn't require a huge boat to get into some fine fishing.

Beginning at Williamstown, there are a host of great fishing opportunities on offer in and around the moored boats and the wharves. A real highlight is casting lightly weighted baits or lures around the mooring chains or shaded boat hulls. Here you will find bream and trevally waiting to grab your offering before trying to breaking you off (and often succeeding!) on the many obstructions close by.

The area known as the Warmies at Newport Power Station and the mouth of the Yarra are both great fishing locations as well, offering a range of species including bream, mullet, trevally and at times good numbers of chopper tailor. Travelling up into the Yarra River, bream are the dominant species but the elusive mulloway is become a popular target. Anglers casting lures around the Punt Road Bridge, Queens Bridge and jetties in the marinas tend to do quite well. Metal vibe lures and soft plastics are deadly during the winter months. The other prized catches that are on offer here at various times are some nice snapper that move around the mouth of the Yarra and towards Princess Pier, as well as some big mulloway—these will also move up and into the channel that heads toward the Newport Power Station.

Throughout the deeper reaches off Williamstown there are good numbers of snapper to be taken, especially in December and then later in the season around February and March.

Heading along the coastline towards St Kilda there are several great piers that anglers can fish from with a very good chance of tangling with some quality fish. One species that is quite popular with land-based anglers is garfish. September is a prime time to catch them as they are usually in plague proportions. A small float setup with size 12 long shank hook works well. Make sure you use berley too. A fine blend of bran or pollard mixed with tuna oil will attract them to your area. Dough, silverfish and maggots make top baits.

WHERE TO FISH – BOAT FISHING

If fishing the area from Station Pier to St Kilda in the boat, you will find some of the best bottom structure is in shallow water ranging from 4 – 9 m. Here the bottom is made up of scattered cunjevoi and mussel beds, both of which create prime feeding grounds for snapper.

The shallow low-lying reefs also hold a reasonable population of fish called ling. While ling are slippery and not very handsome, they do taste great.

Out from St Kilda Marina and up towards North Road boat ramp there is plenty of great snapper ground. The area is famous for the big fish that move into the shallows to feed at night, with some sensational fishing to be had during November and December over the snaggy bottom that ranges from 3 – 6 m deep.

Up towards and past North Road boat ramp the shallow heavy reef is also a top location to find good whiting during the summer and autumn, and while they aren't usually as abundant as further south there are often whiting here over 40 cm. The shallow reefs also abound with squid and garfish.

Outer Macedon

This is still one of the most consistent snapper marks in the top end of the bay. It's comprised of rubble and mussel bottom and at times some excellent catches of snapper are taken here. Best times are November to December. Some nice size gummy sharks have also been taken here in the evening.

The mark is simple to pick up. Looking north about 200 m inside the shipping channel markers, you will see the left hand peak and slope of Mt. Macedon in the distance. Place the peak inside the two main girders of the West Gate Bridge. Looking back across the channel to the Point Cook trees, fit the plantation of trees in the gap between the port and starboard markers directly out from the Marina at St.Kilda.

Inner Macedon

This is well inshore of the Outer Macedon. Hold the same mark with 'The Cook' in the gap between the two channel markers. Looking back to the West Gate Bridge, place the peak on Mt. Macedon on the right hand run up to the bridge.

Small snapper and some whiting are found here, but the main target is big snapper during a heavy onshore blow from the south-west or in the hours of darkness. Sea lice can often ruin a night's fishing here but if they are on holidays, the big reds are usually on the job.

Magpie

About the same distance out as the Kerford Road Pier and 800 m back towards St.Kilda, there is a pole in the water. There used to be a black buoy here that shags and gulls would sit on, hence it was black and white and therefore 'The Magpie'. Some nice whiting move in this area and some good schools of small snapper appear here after Christmas each year. Red mullet, leatherjacket and some squid also make a trip worthwhile.

Caution: Be aware of the yellow buoys that signify the no boating zones. Police patrol the area regularly.

Elwood Drain

During November this spot can be dynamite late at night. While there isn't an exact spot the bottom here is made up of lots of patches of low lying reef. Fish in roughly 5 m of water and most of all keep noise to a minimum. The results here can be outstanding in both numbers and sizes of snapper available.

Outer Elwood

This mark is situated midway between the shore and the shipping channel directly out from the Elwood Canal. Snapper and gummy sharks provide good sport from just prior to Christmas, through to February. Long liners frequently fish this area at this time. Daytime fishing is best because the lice are bad at night if the red weed is on the bottom.

Cement Mark

This is a favourite mark of snapper legend Neil Thompson. It is situated directly out from the Brighton Breakwater where the cement joins the large rocks. It is a clay and shell bottom with some small snapper and flathead a problem at times. However, when a good school of pinkys are in the area, it is hot. Southerlies are best and the spot is only 500 m out from the rock wall.

North Road Whiting Mark

Situated directly out from the North Road ramp and in a line with the end of the Brighton Breakwall is an area that produces some excellent whiting. Good flathead are also taken here in autumn and the occasional school of trevally gives good sport. Some thumping leatherjackets have also been taken here in recent years. Late in September, garfish are also prolific and a lot of fun to catch. A simple berley trail will see them swarm in numbers.

Norwood

This is a famous area off Norwood Avenue, Brighton. To find the area, place the new Fawkner Beacon in the middle of the land mass at Portarlington. Looking north, the St.Kilda Marina lighthouse will split Luna Park. Anglers have had success here for many years, with big snapper to 6 kg and large gummys being the targets here. It is heavy ground with mussels, mud oysters and some reef making an ideal home for the snapper. Best times are late in the afternoon, or just after a strong south-westerly on a change of tide.

Flathead Drift

If you love a feed of flatties, there are some nice sand flathead taken on the drift about 2 km out from the Brighton Breakwall. You can drift using whitebait and pilchard, or another top option is to get hold of a few soft plastic lures. Flathead love them and any pinky snapper in the area also find them hard to resist. Once you find a good patch, either anchor and berley, or drift over the spot again.

Caution: Do not navigate on the shore side of Bonnet Rock between Brighton Pier and Dendy Street. On a very low tide, usually with an offshore wind, you will see exposed reef which can be very hazardous to boats.

Dendy Street Area

Between Bonnet Rock and Green Point at South Road, there are some magnificent whiting and small snapper grounds about 200 m from shore. Garfish are also plentiful in summer and at times there are some excellent flathead taken, especially from February to March when the big females spawn in close. Best results are where you can see the light and dark patches on the bottom. Cast away from the boat and move every fifteen minutes if no bites are felt.

BOAT RAMPS

There are a number of good ramps in this large area.

The Warmies: This has an excellent multi lane concrete ramp with plenty of parking and services the upper end of the Bay, including Hobsons Bay.

St Kilda Marina: This is a totally safe double lane ramp protected from all weather and is serviced by excellent wharves.

North Road: The boat ramp at Brighton at the end of North road is serviceable but exposed in all but easterlies.

WHERE TO FISH – SHORE BASED

Breakwater Pier

A most productive fishing spot for the shore-based angler is the rock wall leading to Breakwater Pier at Williamstown. It is one of the few spots around the bay where you can park your vehicle almost alongside your rods and sit in comfort when the weather is nasty. In fact, the best snapper conditions are when the waves are pounding into the wall from the south or south-west. Large snapper are often taken here in these conditions and on one occasion, three big fish landed here in one hour.

The wall is also popular with whiting anglers and good numbers of fish are taken fishing early morning, evening and at night. Reasonable numbers of flathead are also caught, which can at times be frustrating for those anglers concentrating on the whiting.

Station Pier

This is where the Spirit of Tasmania passenger ferry departs, and the pier is in deep water. It can turn up a variety of species at any time from bream and trevally in close to the pylons, through to mulloway, salmon and snapper on larger baits cast out from the pier. During winter it also tends to produce good numbers of pinky snapper.

St Kilda Breakwall and Pier

A popular spot due to its central location, the pier always has someone fishing from it for species such as garfish and small salmon, while a larger bait cast out over the relatively shallow and sandy bottom sees the odd nice flathead taken. At times, baits fished close to the pylons can attract good bream during summer and trevally in winter.

Fishing from the breakwall itself produces garfish and flathead; however during October, November and December at night (and especially in rough weather) anglers can find some great fishing for big snapper and the odd decent gummy shark.

Lagoon Pier

While it doesn't protrude into the bay as far as Station Pier, Lagoon Pier is a noted spot for anglers to target large mulloway at night during April, May and June with live baits of mullet suspended under floats.

Kerford Road Jetty

This jetty is easy to access thanks to a tram line passing close by. It produces good catches of garfish, mullet and some small salmon at times for anglers fishing with floats.

There are also some very good whiting to be taken here early morning and late in the afternoon along with squid. However if larger fish are your choice then fishing here at night or during rough weather in November and December can produce some very nice snapper.

Brighton Pier

This is one of the best land based locations along this stretch of coastline and it consistently produces good fishing and great fish.

The broken ground that is scattered along the breakwall's length produces good numbers of squid and garfish, while casting larger baits out into deeper water can produce good numbers of pinky snapper, salmon, and some gummy sharks especially in late autumn and winter.

During October, November and December fishing at night along the breakwall from the bend to the end is a top way catch some big snapper—especially when a strong south-wester is blowing.

Aside from the baitfishing opportunities, land based anglers are now finding great success working along the outside of the breakwall using light spin rods and casting soft plastic lures for pinky snapper. There are even some much bigger snapper being taken from time to time on lures.

Along the inside of the pier and breakwall there is also good fishing to be had for anglers chasing mullet, trevally and some very big bream, especially if you cast baits and lures in close proximity to the moored boats and pylons.

The Gully

The Gully has been a famous spot for many years, especially for catching big snapper after the dark or during a strong blow from the south west. There are also good catches of rock flathead at times and trevally and whiting. The Gully runs about 250 m offshore between the Hampton Life Saving Club and New Street railway crossing.

New Street Groyne

Built in 1988 to reduce erosion, this groyne has been a real gem for shore-based anglers. It offers some hope for snapper anglers at night as the waters of 'The Gully' are not far away. The rock groynes jut out far enough into the bay to put land based anglers in reach of some red hot fishing. Even though The Gully is so close to shore, good numbers of snapper move in here in season, especially during or after a strong south west wind. During winter the same ground is excellent for pinky snapper.

Other species available are whiting, which can be taken in good numbers during summer and autumn, as well as garfish and squid. The broken bottom also brings less common species into this area from time to time with the odd report of school mulloway being caught.

Dendy Street

The shallow areas here are frequented by garfish anglers in summer and quite a number wade the area spreading bread crumbs in search of the large 'nobby' gars that swim around this very heavy reef. North winds are good and easterly winds most certainly are worth the effort.

RIGHT: Big reds are a common catch if you know where to look.

CHAPTER 7
SANDRINGHAM TO MORDIALLOC
MAP 10

This stretch of the bay consistently produces great fishing all year round for just about every species of fish that can be taken in the waters of Port Phillip Bay. Pinky-sized to monster snapper, whiting, salmon, trevally, leatherjacket, snook, red mullet, garfish and squid are caught here to name a few. This area is also one of the better places to find yellowtail kingfish, which are becoming more common each summer.

Part of the appeal of this area is the large, solid reef systems that abound along the coastline. Best of all, many of these reefs start at the shore and taper into the water before dropping off quickly. This allows fish to sit in deeper water during non-feeding periods, and then move only a short distance to the prime feeding grounds. In addition to the reefs, there is some excellent man-made structure in the form of the mussel farms found out from the Beaumaris Motor Yacht Squadron in Beaumaris Bay. These hanging structures are great locations for many species.

Boat access to this stretch of coastline is catered for by several ramps. The closest ramp is at Half Moon Bay, which is often shallow and difficult to use. Nevertheless it's usually okay for boats up to 5.5m, except during northerly winds. There is a private ramp at Beaumaris Motor Yacht Squadron for members only, and then another public ramp up in Mordialloc Creek. The ramp itself is a good one—the only thing that stops it from being more popular is that boats must pass under the Nepean Highway bridge which is quite low. In saying that, most half cabin boats up to or just over 6 m can get under it, although it may be necessary to fold canopies and rocket launchers down. As for the entrance to the creek itself, it is quite narrow and does at times get shallow, however it is dredged fairly regularly so you can get in and out on all tides.

The general area abounds in rich reef, weed and sandy patches. The reef area between Sandringham and Mordialloc is a marvellous haven for fish. Species caught or seen caught include snapper, King George whiting, flathead, trevally, warehou, butterfish (dusky morwong), flounder, garfish, spotted ling, zebra fish, rock cod, Australian salmon, snook, gummy shark, yellowtail kingfish, tailor, senator wrasse, red mullet, parrot fish and six varieties of leatherjacket.

The two mussel farms adjacent to `Keefers' have added structure to the area, with the shells growing on suspended ropes acting as an artificial reef.

BOAT FISHING – WHERE TO FISH

Yorkies Reef

This is a wide patch of reef, kelp, weed and shell covering a broad area between Bay Road and the eastern edge of the Sandringham Breakwater. There have been many good days of fishing here and sometimes before and after dark, the snapper fishing can be excellent. The area is about as big as a football ground with prime spots about 250 to 400 m from shore.

Throughout the summer months Yorkies Reef is a very consistent whiting spot, especially early morning and late afternoon. Sometimes it takes a few moves around the reef to find the whiting, and while pipis can be good bait, generally there is better success with mussels.

During autumn and winter this area is a top spot to find pinky snapper. It is now regarded as a prime location to lure fishing for pinkys with soft plastic lures, especially late in the afternoon or when there has been a bit of rough weather to stir up the water.

Anonyma Shoal

This shallow reef ledge area was once marked by an unlit green buoy. After several near misses by craft and one direct hit by one well known angler, the buoy was replaced by Cardinal markers. The reef itself is located about 2 km out from Bay Road and is a very productive fishing ground.

Being situated where the reef system comes from roughly 8 m of water up to within 2 m of the surface, makes it a great fishing spot, although it is amazing that more fishermen don't fish here.

As for fishing options, it is a fine spot to troll lures around the reef edge for some very big snook, as well as being a good area to find salmon and barracouta, especially during spring and autumn.

During the summer months whiting are usually taken here in good numbers, as well as garfish. When gars turn up in the berley, it's worth putting one out live as the Anonyma Shoal is also a top spot to find yellowtail kingfish. As each year passes, more and more kingies come into the bay to harass the whiting and garfish anglers.

The outside edge of the reef is also a good place to find big snapper in October and November, especially before first light.

Red Buoy – Black Rock

Out from the Half Moon Bay Boat ramp there is a red yachting buoy that sits in about 13 m of water. While there is no real structure, the area for half a kilometre around it is an excellent place to find big snapper, especially during the morning or in periods of rough weather.

Small snapper are prevalent at most times of the year but the peak is usually from February to Easter. As the reef is very heavy, it's preferable to fish unweighted baits such as pilchards or garfish fillets

The drop-off to the mud area outside the pylon is an excellent early season snapper mark. A rising or steady barometer after a very heavy south-west blow is the recipe for bag limit catches.

Red Bluff Mark

Situated as the name suggests off the Red Bluff Hotel, this feature is about 200 m offshore and runs for some distance south to north. A combination of rock, reef, weed and shell banks, the area is renowned for excellent catches of small snapper after dark. The whiting here, while not thick are quite large. Some good sized calamari squid have been taken here. Using a pellet type berley early in the fishing session, will assist in the attraction of small fish and then other targeted fish like snapper, whiting and trevally will move in.

Fish just on the drop-off from the ledge into the gutter that runs adjacent to the shore. There are some heavy weed patches between here and the Cerberus Wreck in Half Moon Bay which are always worth a cast for whiting. One major problem that will have to be addressed is the traffic from jet skis during hot weather and calm seas.

Cerberus Mark

This mark is often overlooked by anglers keen to go deep. A close study of the bottom about 50 m due west of the wreck will reveal quite a steep reef area which is well worth a look—especially just before dark for snapper. Anglers can do really well here early in the season. It is also an area that holds an amazing number of leatherjacket.

It is worth sounding over this reef, which runs to the north, as there are some reasonable sized holes and dips that hold good whiting around dawn and dusk. This is also a top reef to drift over and cast soft plastic lures for pinky snapper during autumn and winter.

Clocktower Reef

This reef is quite famous and is found about 400 m offshore from the clocktower at Balcombe Road. Although it gets anglers fishing on it almost daily it consistently produces great catches of pinky snapper, whiting and red mullet and is nowadays a favoured spot for anglers to fish with soft plastic lures for pinky snapper during the winter months.

Not surprisingly, with the last few years producing excellent snapper seasons generally, this reef has been producing some much bigger snapper on more than the odd occasion.

One good tip here is to fish for the pinkys on this reef in the afternoon. As they go off the bite start to move closer to shore—you will find the pinkys moving into shallower water as it gets dark.

Marine Park

Moving along the coast towards Ricketts Point, yellow marker buoys and signs mark the boundary of a marine park which stretches roughly from Fourth Street to the Scout Hall in Beaumaris Bay. Take note where the boundaries are, as fishing in the park will see you fined.

Throughout winter, anglers flicking soft plastics work the outer side of the markers to produce some very impressive snapper. Fishing first light throughout the winter months is the prime time.

Huge schools of salmon are also prolific at this time and tend to "bust up" on the surface around a tide change. Once again, those casting soft plastic lures will have plenty of fun catching and releasing these magnificent sportfish. This location isn't too far from shore either, and those fishing from kayak's can also get into the action with a short paddle from the Beaumaris boat ramp.

Rubble Ground

A very good big snapper mark especially early in the season around October and November. The ground is not sharply defined but about 4 km out from the Balcombe clocktower there are several yachting buoys which help to locate it. The ground is fairly general through here so snapper will often be scattered over a wide area, so often there can be good results by finding one or two fish on the sounder, then anchoring and using berley to attract a school of fish.

This is an area favoured by many Beaumaris anglers producing good snapper catches both early morning and late afternoon.

2 Fingers Mark

In front of the Ricketts Point Teahouse and out in 16 m of water, is a great early season snapper mark called 2 Fingers. Here two natural lumps create structure on a relatively featureless bottom. For best results it generally pays to fish just up-tide of the lumps, allowing berley and baits to go back toward the structure.

The GPS mark for 2 Fingers is:
S 37 59 461
E 144 59 142

Table Rock Drop-Off

This is a good early season mark for medium size snapper and is found about 90 m due south of Table Rock. Most fishable nights during the season you will see the lights of boats fishing here.

This is also a good salmon spot, and some monster whiting (for this area) of nearly 800 gm have been taken. A slight southerly sea breeze with clear skies creates ideal fishing conditions. Snapper are best late afternoon or before sun-up.

The line of pylons here are all cardinal marks. Inside the sticks there is very shallow and uneven reef formations that can be very dangerous to unsuspecting boat operators.

Mussel Farm

This area is easily found as it lies just offshore from Beaumaris Pier and is visible via yellow markers as well as the black balls and drums that indicate the actual mussel farm.

Fishing around the outside of the farm—especially on the deep water side—produces good pinky fishing during autumn and winter, and some good snapper at night in October.

Casting soft plastic lures amongst the farm at times produces good catches of snotty trevalla, salmon, silver trevally and pinkys.

Gasso Mark

Out off Ricketts Point in 18 m of water lies a large gas line that runs along the bottom. It is shown on maps and many GPS systems, and while it is covered by mud it does create a slight rise in the bottom.

This area is one of the top snapper areas in the bay, producing big numbers and big fish. Best of all, it often fishes best from mid morning to late afternoon, and some of the largest catches are taken by those anglers who anchor up and stay in the one spot. When the snapper arrive, it's often the whole school and every rod takes off.

The Gasso is a general area with little bottom structure, so if you sound one fish, anchor up—it will usually have plenty of mates around.

GPS coordinates:
S -38 01 981
E -144 58 070

Pizza Mark Mentone

This area is a very good snapper spot where anglers have consistently caught fish when things are tough elsewhere. It is about 3 km straight out from the old Mentone Pier but due to the peninsula-like makeup of the shore running from Beaumaris Bay to Ricketts Point, the spot is also only a kilometre out from Table Rock.

To pick up the mark looking north-east into shore, line up the cathedral on top of Kilbreda School at Mentone and place it in the middle of the pizza shop just to the right of the Mentone Lifesaving Club. Looking north, split the rocks at Quiet Corner in the middle of the West Gate Bridge. October and November are top months here and good catches of large snapper have been taken in the middle of the day.

Horse Paddock

The area known as the `Horse Paddock' used to be a popular venue to swim race horses after they did track work at nearby Epsom Racecourse at Mordialloc. This area has been assisted by sand dredging and replenishment of the beach between Mentone and Mordialloc. The moving sand has exposed reef normally hidden under silt from Mordialloc Creek. This exposed reef has grown weed and attracted minute food which, in turn, has attracted fish like snapper and whiting. While the reef isn't as noticeable as around areas like Ricketts Point, during the summer months whiting fishers regularly have their fish harassed by schools of kingfish, which for some reason like holding in this area.

Parkdale Pinnacles

Not unlike the Anonyma Shoal, the reef system off Sandringham known as the Parkdale Pinnacles is a heavy reef system lying out from the shore. It comes up from 6 – 8 m of water to within 2 m of the surface in certain areas, and produces good fishing all year round.

Fishing here in September often sees anglers landing big

Catching Big Snapper is the pinnacle of fishing the Bay.

snapper amongst the smaller pinkys, which tends to herald the beginning of the upcoming snapper season.

During October and November good catches of snapper can also be taken here by fishing the outside or deeper edges of the reef in low light and rough conditions, while summer catches include pinkys and whiting

Caution: An area that should be navigated with care is the shelf directly in front of the Red Bluff Hotel. It is about 120 m out and is very shallow at low tide. The area around the Anonyma Shoal can also be a hazard to boats drawing deep water (displacement hulls). It is also renowned for deep crevices and the loss of anchors can be a problem.

The rocky ledge running toward the Cerberus Breakwater from the Black Rock ramp has also claimed many boat propellers. There is a small channel in between the shore and the Cerberus but anglers unfamiliar with the area would be best advised to go around the Port Melbourne or seaward side of the Cerberus.

A hazard which should be rectified is the problem of unlit pylons and buoys in the area. It is wise to make a mental note as to the location of these nasty traps before the sun sets.

The dark of night and the silhouettes of the pylons make it very hard to distinguish where they are, you can be concentrating on the pylons and run right into an unlit yachting buoy. The best advice is don't fish after dark unless you are very familiar with the area.

Drifting and Lure Fishing

Drifting through this whole reef system, especially along the front of the marine park from Ricketts Point down to Black Rock, is a very popular way to fish these days during autumn and winter. Many anglers are doing away with the usual bait fishing methods for pinkys, instead using light spinning tackle and soft plastic lures. They are catching more and bigger fish than ever and having an absolute ball doing it. The other bonus when drift fishing with the lures is the amount of water you can cove, helping you find the fish faster, as well as locating other species that are also keen to eat a lure such as salmon, red mullet and snook.

BOAT RAMPS

Sandringham Yacht Club: A private ramp only and not open to public.
Beaumaris Motor Yacht Squad Club: A private ramp only and not open to public.
Half Moon Bay: The public ramp at Black Rock is a single lane concrete but is exposed in rough weather.
Pompie: A private concrete ramp in Mordialloc creek open to the public, located on beach road.
Mordialloc Creek: Upstream of Pompie and on Govenor Road, a good twin concrete ramp. A bit shallow downstream on low tides.

SHORE BASED FISHING

Beaumaris Pier

One of the best places to target squid land based, this pier fishes well for squid for several months of the year, especially late in the afternoon.

It is fairly protected in south-west winds and completely calm in any sort of northerly, so it is a popular spot for many anglers and especially kids on school holidays.

As for other fishing options, the pier produces good numbers of whiting and garfish during summer, pinkys and flathead during autumn and winter, and some great snapper in spring – especially in rough weather. Anglers keen on catching big snapper fish from the pier in very strong westerly and south westerly winds. The pier is quite small and can only cope with two or four anglers all fishing at the same time. Get there early and you'll get a good spot.

When salmon are about, the schools will often push bait into the area around the pier, giving anglers great sport with lures.

Mordialloc Pier

This is where Rex Hunt learnt to fish. Famous pier names like Alec Rowe, Roy Selleck and Harold George were his heroes. Garfish and trevally were his speciality along the pier, and mullet and bream at the mouth of the Mordialloc Creek. On Christmas Eve of 1963, he took a snapper of 3 kg off the end of the pier on a Crouch reel.

More recently, local hero Jack Pompei helped saved the pier from a severe shortening, and it remains very popular with young anglers.

Mordialloc Creek itself, while still a long way from being pristine, is better than it used to be. It actually clears up enough after periods of no rain that you can see the bottom.

The fishing in the creek is quite good, especially in autumn and winter for big mullet and small salmon, which are taken using baits of maggots and dough suspended under floats. There are also some huge bream that live in the creek which are very hard to catch. However if you can get hold of some shrimp for bait you may find yourself trying to stop a rampaging bream from breaking you off on a mooring.

Fishing along the pier from the creek mouth to the end produces good fishing for mullet, trevally and especially garfish when using floats and baits of maggots, silverfish and dough. Larger baits cast out into the deeper water towards the end of the pier can put you in with a chance of pinkys, salmon and flathead. And if you can handle the awful conditions during a strong south-west wind in November, fishing at the end of the pier can produce some good snapper. During these uncomfortable conditions, it isn't uncommon to witness anglers catch snapper to five kilos or more. Dedication and persistence pays off and when it is rough, this pier can really fire.

As you walk onto the pier, the patch of reef that is on the right hand side of the pier and extends out to past the shelter shed is a great place to fish for squid and whiting during first and last light.

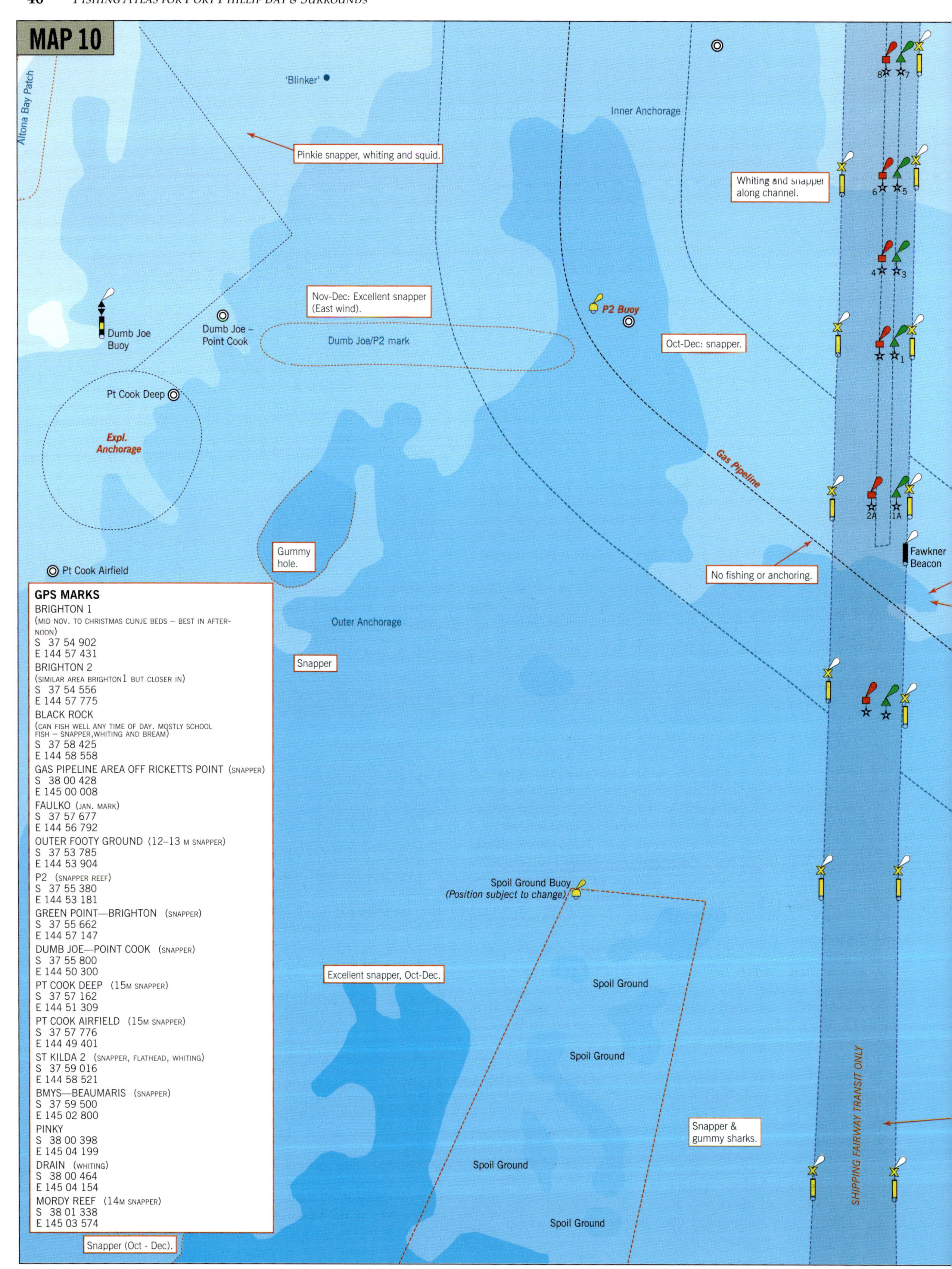
MAP 10
Altona Bay Patch
'Blinker'
Inner Anchorage
Pinkie snapper, whiting and squid.
Whiting and snapper along channel.
8
7
6
5
4
3
2
1
Nov-Dec: Excellent snapper (East wind).
P2 Buoy
Dumb Joe Buoy
Dumb Joe – Point Cook
Dumb Joe/P2 mark
Oct-Dec: snapper.
Pt Cook Deep
Expl. Anchorage
Gas Pipeline
2A
1A
Gummy hole.
Fawkner Beacon
Pt Cook Airfield
No fishing or anchoring.
Outer Anchorage
Snapper
GPS MARKS
BRIGHTON 1
(MID NOV. TO CHRISTMAS CUNJE BEDS – BEST IN AFTER-NOON)
S 37 54 902
E 144 57 431
BRIGHTON 2
(SIMILAR AREA BRIGHTON1 BUT CLOSER IN)
S 37 54 556
E 144 57 775
BLACK ROCK
(CAN FISH WELL ANY TIME OF DAY. MOSTLY SCHOOL FISH – SNAPPER, WHITING AND BREAM)
S 37 58 425
E 144 58 558
GAS PIPELINE AREA OFF RICKETTS POINT (SNAPPER)
S 38 00 428
E 145 00 008
FAULKO (JAN. MARK)
S 37 57 677
E 144 56 792
OUTER FOOTY GROUND (12–13 M SNAPPER)
S 37 53 785
E 144 53 904
P2 (SNAPPER REEF)
S 37 55 380
E 144 53 181
GREEN POINT—BRIGHTON (SNAPPER)
S 37 55 662
E 144 57 147
DUMB JOE—POINT COOK (SNAPPER)
S 37 55 800
E 144 50 300
PT COOK DEEP (15M SNAPPER)
S 37 57 162
E 144 51 309
PT COOK AIRFIELD (15M SNAPPER)
S 37 57 776
E 144 49 401
ST KILDA 2 (SNAPPER, FLATHEAD, WHITING)
S 37 59 016
E 144 58 521
BMYS—BEAUMARIS (SNAPPER)
S 37 59 500
E 145 02 800
PINKY
S 38 00 398
E 145 04 199
DRAIN (WHITING)
S 38 00 464
E 145 04 154
MORDY REEF (14M SNAPPER)
S 38 01 338
E 145 03 574
Spoil Ground Buoy
(Position subject to change).
Excellent snapper, Oct-Dec.
Spoil Ground
Spoil Ground
Spoil Ground
Spoil Ground
Snapper & gummy sharks.
SHIPPING FAIRWAY TRANSIT ONLY
Snapper (Oct - Dec).

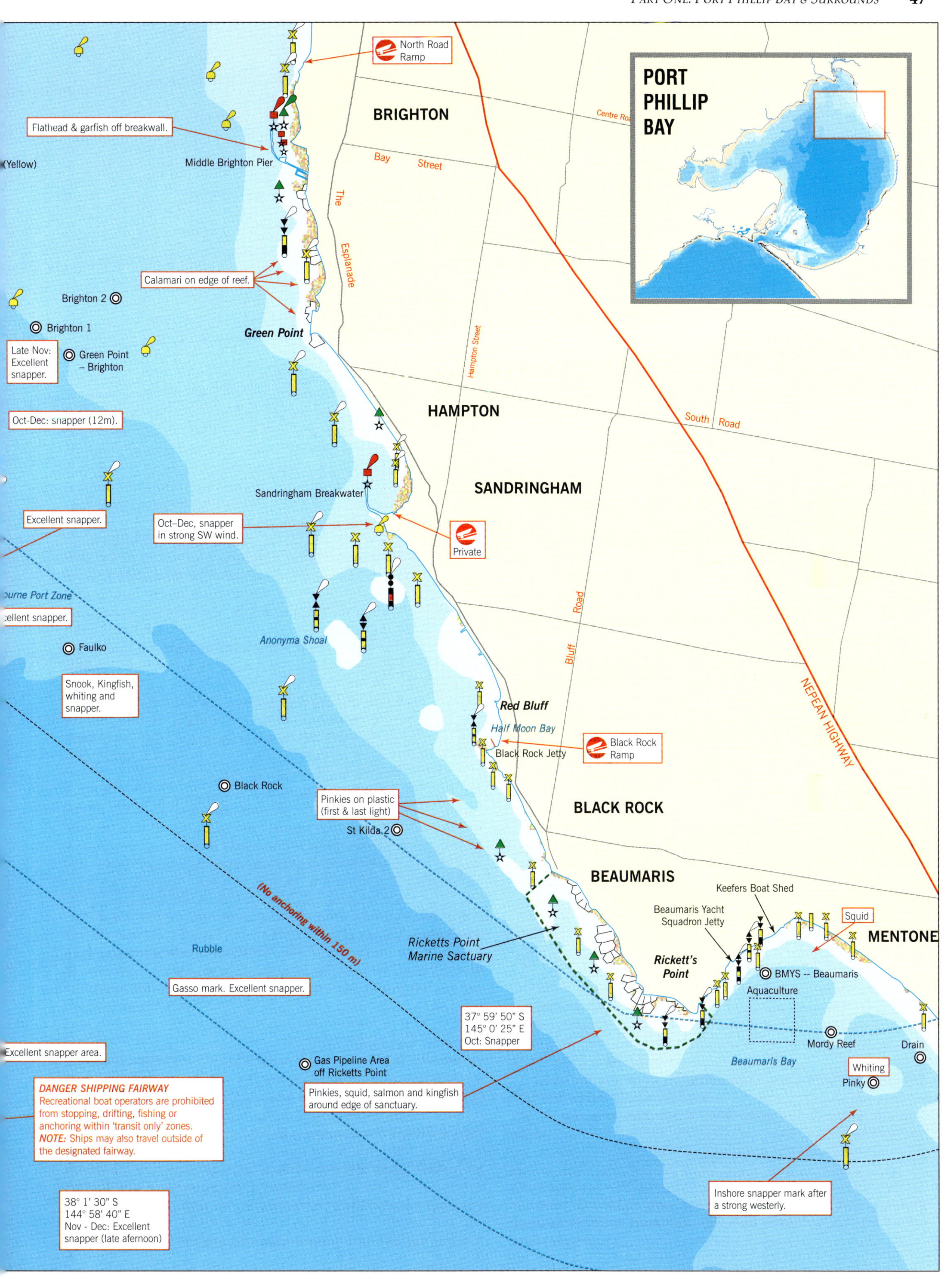

PORT PHILLIP BAY
North Road Ramp
BRIGHTON
Centre Road
Bay Street
The Esplanade
Flathead & garfish off breakwall.
(Yellow)
Middle Brighton Pier
Calamari on edge of reef.
Brighton 2
Brighton 1
Green Point
Late Nov: Excellent snapper.
Green Point – Brighton
Hampton Street
HAMPTON
South Road
Oct-Dec: snapper (12m).
SANDRINGHAM
Sandringham Breakwater
Excellent snapper.
Oct–Dec, snapper in strong SW wind.
Private
urne Port Zone
cellent snapper.
Faulko
Anonyma Shoal
Bluff Road
Snook, Kingfish, whiting and snapper.
Red Bluff
Half Moon Bay
Black Rock Jetty
Black Rock Ramp
NEPEAN HIGHWAY
Black Rock
Pinkies on plastic (first & last light)
St Kilda 2
BLACK ROCK
BEAUMARIS
Keefers Boat Shed
Beaumaris Yacht Squadron Jetty
Squid
MENTONE
(No anchoring within 150 m)
Ricketts Point Marine Sactuary
Rickett's Point
BMYS -- Beaumaris
Aquaculture
Rubble
Gasso mark. Excellent snapper.
37° 59' 50" S
145° 0' 25" E
Oct: Snapper
Mordy Reef
Drain
Excellent snapper area.
Gas Pipeline Area off Ricketts Point
Beaumaris Bay
Whiting
Pinky
DANGER SHIPPING FAIRWAY
Recreational boat operators are prohibited from stopping, drifting, fishing or anchoring within 'transit only' zones.
NOTE: Ships may also travel outside of the designated fairway.
Pinkies, squid, salmon and kingfish around edge of sanctuary.
Inshore snapper mark after a strong westerly.
38° 1' 30" S
144° 58' 40" E
Nov - Dec: Excellent snapper (late afernoon)

CHAPTER 8
MORDIALLOC TO FRANKSTON
MAPS 11

Since the removal of the scallop dredges, which used to work this area extensively, the fishing in this part of the bay has rejuvenated. It now sees a large amount of angling effort each year, as big schools of snapper move in to this part of the bay to feed and spawn. What's more, anglers are well catered for with good boat ramps at Mordialloc Creek, Patterson River and Kananook Creek at Frankston. These ramps are all in close proximity to rich snapper grounds.

The make-up of the bottom in this area is similar to the majority of Port Phillip Bay as it shelves gently with a soft mud substrate. However in amongst the mud are patches of scallops, mussels and small areas of gravel, all of which provide the ideal environment for snapper. Meanwhile the crab population is increasing again out on the mud bottom, creating great fishing in areas that were once barren due to the scallop dredges.

Adding to the natural structure, this part of the bay also features three artificial reefs that were placed in the bay to help promote the fishery. To this day these reefs are popular spots that produce some great snapper fishing each year.

The Patterson River, which is covered in the estuary section of this book, is a delightful waterway. This river proves when development is mixed with the right amount of nature, the result can be a terrific piscatorial environment. The river mouth is the gateway to marvellous fishing in season (November to April).

BOAT FISHING – WHERE TO FISH

THE WELL

`The Well' was named by Black Rock tackle man; the late John Wright and his mate Keith Clayton. The story goes that John and Keith were having a horrid season some years ago. They decided to run the boat out of Mordialloc Creek until the petrol left in one of the tanks ran out. They did this and dropped onto a heap of feeding snapper. Each time they returned they did well so they called the mark `The Well' because they kept on going back to it.

The Well is located about 2 km off Edithvale. To locate the mark, look north-east and place the main Monash University building in the middle of the clump of cypress trees on the shore. Now looking north, you will see the main spire of Kilbreda College at Mentone— place this on the end of Mordialloc Pier.

On the seaward side of the mussel beds there is a large area of rubble. This comprises of clay, shell grit, spent scallop and mussel shells, clumps of blue mussels and mud oysters and a fair coverage of mud. Once again this is prime snapper territory.

While anglers love to have their `secret' marks, there is no need here. Just look to see where the boats are congregated and you will know where they have been getting the fish.

At times when the south or westerly blow increases the sea swell, some lovely gummy sharks have been caught over the mussels, also snapper within 300 m of the shore at times in the rough.

MORDIALLOC REEF

This is a rather large patch of scattered reef south and south-east of the Mordialloc Pier. It is popular with hire craft from Mordialloc Creek and at times is very productive for small snapper and some large flathead. In the months of November and December, there are many good snapper taken here just after a blow.

On days when it is sunny and the wind is from the north or the east, you can see the dark outline of the reef area clearly. These conditions do not happen regularly so it might be best to take a shore mark to ensure you can find your spot next time.

While the reef lies in relatively shallow water it does produce good fishing for pinky snapper and the odd bigger fish during the season. It is also a good spot to berley for the gars which tend to hang around the reef. The last few summers have also seen decent numbers of yakkas and slimy mackerel taken here from time to time.

MUSSEL BEDS

About 200 m out from shore, there is a line of mussel beds that go right along the area from Aspendale to Seaford. During onshore winds, good hauls of snapper are caught here from September to December. Gummy sharks are also caught in the area just before and after dark; however sea lice can be a problem at times.

INNER ARTIFICIAL REEF

This artificial reef is marked by a large yellow buoy and is located in 10 m of water off Aspendale. It was built in 1973, and is made up of bunches of tyres that have been bound together. This spot fishes well at first and last light, especially after several days of strong winds

There has also been an odd school mulloway (about 3 kg) caught here by snapper fishermen. If you're coming out from Carrum, the buoy marking the reef is located around 5 km in a line towards Ricketts Point.

GPS Coordinates:

OUTER ARTIFICIAL REEF

The second and possibly the most popular reef is known as the Outer Artificial and is located roughly 6 km off Chelsea. It produces snapper consistently throughout the season, and it is also known for producing some good mulloway during January and February. This reef was created by an old barge and although there isn't a lot of it left, it is still a great spot.

This area should be happily re-named "the Paddock" due to the large amounts of boats that sit in the area throughout the season. Though it is a productive location for snapper, it isn't uncommon to see fifty or more boats sitting around it at any one time.

GPS coordinates:
S 38 04.701
E 145 02.339

IN CLOSE CHELSEA TO SEAFORD

In close to shore in this area is good to work when the water is very coloured. Big snapper love foraging here after a big blow. However novice boat handlers be warned that fishing close to shore in a very heavy sea can be hazardous, and should only be attempted by experienced seamen.

The reason the snapper move into the area is because of the

heavy cunjevoi growth on the bottom in which snapper feed amongst. In rough weather, the bottom is stirred up sending potential foods throughout the water columns.

Riviera Hotel Mark

This is a broad area that produces many large snapper every year. After heavy onshore seas, the water becomes discoloured and the fish can bite during the day. Red weed is a problem here at times so constant checking of baits is essential for good results. The area is about 1.5 km straight out from the Riviera Hotel at Seaford, adjacent to the Eel Race Drain structure.

Mile Bridge

Situated midway between the piers at Seaford and Frankston, this is a famous area especially with Frankston anglers. Although calm conditions rarely produce results here, it seems every time we have a huge blow from the south-west between November and December, someone gets into the Mile Bridge mark area and has a ball. Once again it is quite heavy ground with lots of clumps of mussels and red weed.

Many people have their own secret Mile Bridge mark, however there is lots of scattered reef in water depths from 7-10m, with 8 m being a favourite, so it often pays to use the sounder to find some reef or fish before anchoring. Fishing the area on first light is the key in shallow water and by sunrise the fish will move out into deeper water.

After a strong south westerly blow, fishing in close from Mornington to Carrum can be very successful.

The Wreck

Many years ago a ship sank about 2 km off Frankston and to this day the location is simply known as the Wreck. It lies in about 11m of water and although not always a consistent spot, it does produce some very big snapper. It's also a popular spot for lure anglers who take some good fish from this area.

To locate the reef, look over the end of the Frankston Pier and line up the Bowling Club building with the extreme end point of the pier. Then looking north to Mt Dandenong, move until the peak where the television towers are located goes over the end of the Seaford Pier.

The Wreck fishes best during a strong westerly blow and up to two days after the blow. Berleying is a good method to aid in bringing the fish on the bite.

GPS co-ordinates:
S 38 08.045
E 145 05.855

Outer Seaford

This mark is located about 3 km out directly in line with the Seaford Pier. If you look back towards Mt Eliza, you will see a distinct yellow / orange section of the cliff face (hard to see in the morning) and on top of the hill is a green water tower. If you line up the tower and the cliff, you will be over a very good productive spot for snapper and large flathead. There are also some big catches of gars taken here after Christmas.

Inner Seaford

Seaford is a large area to fish but in around 16 meters of water, the bottom is thick cunjevoi which invites snapper to the area. Plenty of snapper area taken here with the prime months being October and November. Anglers fishing first light do very well then they tend to move out deeper as the sun rises. The best fishing is two days after a strong westerly blow.

GPS co-ordinates:
S 38 06.761
E 145 03.90

Hospital Mark

This is more of an area than a specific mark and for whatever reason it tends to concentrate large schools of snapper each season. It is usually quite easy to find as there always seems to be a few boats in the area.

The bottom here is about 16 m deep and is mostly made up of mud, scallops and mussels, although these days many anglers have added to the bottom structure by making there own secret artificial reefs. While these are quite small they do fish well for snapper

GPS coordinates:
S -38 08 816
E -145 02 188

BOAT RAMPS

Carrum (Patterson River): A very modern and well laid out launching area is reached by driving down McLeod Road from either Wells Road or the Nepean Highway. Turn down Launching Way and the ramp is reached by driving past the kiosk and over the hill. Four double ramps and parking for over 200 cars and trailers cater well for the boating angler. The ramps can take boats up to 7 m in length. The complex is financed by a number of organisations within the Dandenong Valley Authority Management Committee.

The River mouth is dredged regularly allowing for safe passage of large and long drawing vessels. At times, the dredge may be operating during the day and night. Refer to boating regulations regarding identification signs and flags on the unit.

Frankston (Kananook Creek): This near perfect launching ramp located near the foot of the Frankston Pier takes six boats at a time. Although the water near the ramp is quite deep, caution is needed near the creek mouth as a narrow bar section has very little water over it even at high tide. On numerous occasions you can see people outside their boats pushing the hulls over this shallow bar. It is particularly hazardous during a northerly wind exceeding 10 knots.

Frankston (Olivers Hill): This ramp is located at the foot of Olivers Hill just off the intersection of the Nepean Highway with

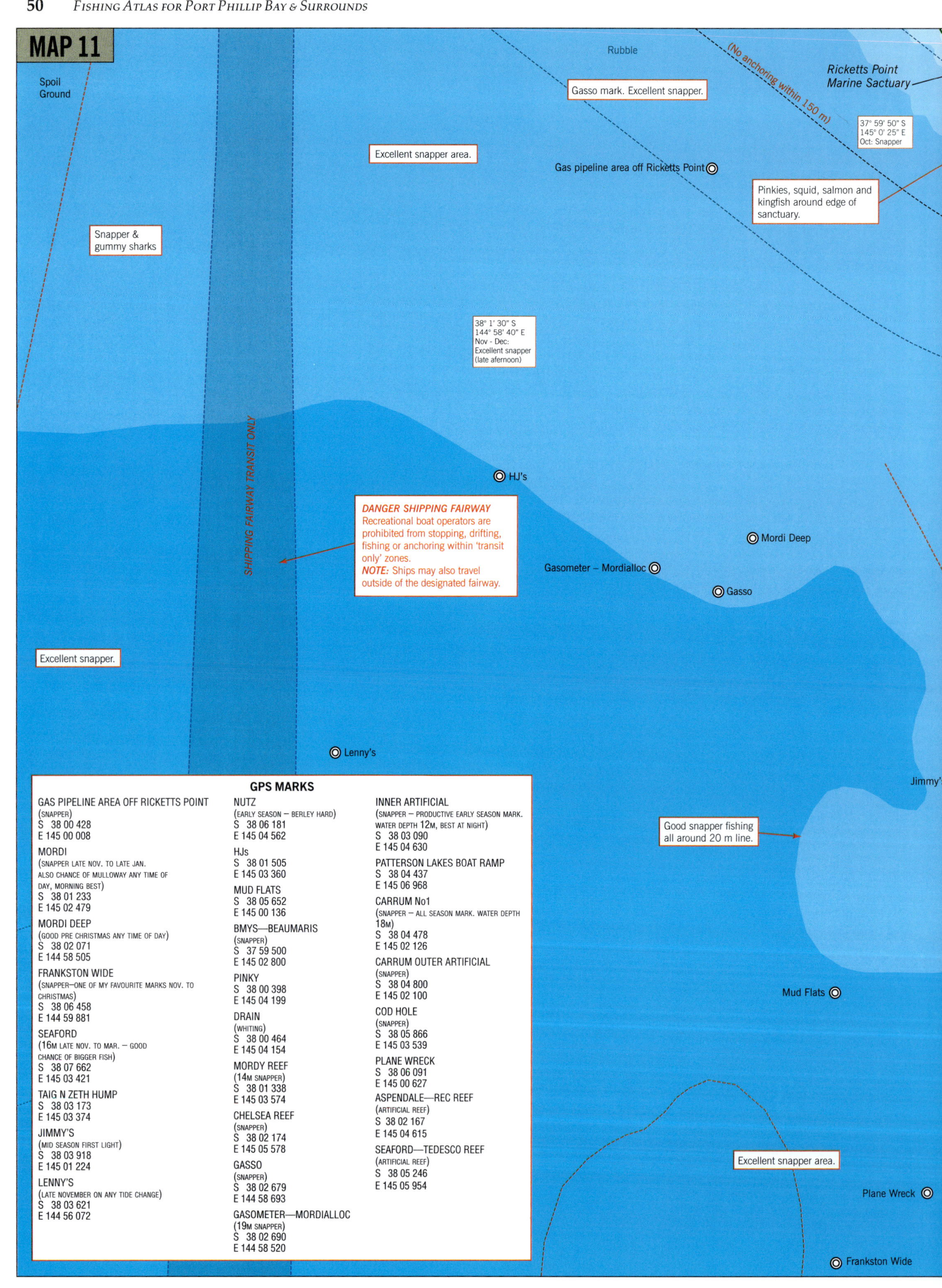
MAP 11
Spoil Ground
Rubble
Gasso mark. Excellent snapper.
(No anchoring within 150 m)
Ricketts Point Marine Sactuary
37° 59' 50" S
145° 0' 25" E
Oct: Snapper
Excellent snapper area.
Gas pipeline area off Ricketts Point
Pinkies, squid, salmon and kingfish around edge of sanctuary.
Snapper & gummy sharks
38° 1' 30" S
144° 58' 40" E
Nov - Dec:
Excellent snapper
(late afernoon)
SHIPPING FAIRWAY TRANSIT ONLY
HJ's
DANGER SHIPPING FAIRWAY
Recreational boat operators are prohibited from stopping, drifting, fishing or anchoring within 'transit only' zones.
NOTE: Ships may also travel outside of the designated fairway.
Mordi Deep
Gasometer – Mordialloc
Gasso
Excellent snapper.
Lenny's
Jimmy's
Good snapper fishing all around 20 m line.
Mud Flats
Excellent snapper area.
Plane Wreck
Frankston Wide
GPS MARKS
GAS PIPELINE AREA OFF RICKETTS POINT
(SNAPPER)
S 38 00 428
E 145 00 008
MORDI
(SNAPPER LATE NOV. TO LATE JAN. ALSO CHANCE OF MULLOWAY ANY TIME OF DAY, MORNING BEST)
S 38 01 233
E 145 02 479
MORDI DEEP
(GOOD PRE CHRISTMAS ANY TIME OF DAY)
S 38 02 071
E 144 58 505
FRANKSTON WIDE
(SNAPPER—ONE OF MY FAVOURITE MARKS NOV. TO CHRISTMAS)
S 38 06 458
E 144 59 881
SEAFORD
(16M LATE NOV. TO MAR. – GOOD CHANCE OF BIGGER FISH)
S 38 07 662
E 145 03 421
TAIG N ZETH HUMP
S 38 03 173
E 145 03 374
JIMMY'S
(MID SEASON FIRST LIGHT)
S 38 03 918
E 145 01 224
LENNY'S
(LATE NOVEMBER ON ANY TIDE CHANGE)
S 38 03 621
E 144 56 072
NUTZ
(EARLY SEASON – BERLEY HARD)
S 38 06 181
E 145 04 562
HJs
S 38 01 505
E 145 03 360
MUD FLATS
S 38 05 652
E 145 00 136
BMYS—BEAUMARIS
(SNAPPER)
S 37 59 500
E 145 02 800
PINKY
S 38 00 398
E 145 04 199
DRAIN
(WHITING)
S 38 00 464
E 145 04 154
MORDY REEF
(14M SNAPPER)
S 38 01 338
E 145 03 574
CHELSEA REEF
(SNAPPER)
S 38 02 174
E 145 05 578
GASSO
(SNAPPER)
S 38 02 679
E 144 58 693
GASOMETER—MORDIALLOC
(19M SNAPPER)
S 38 02 690
E 144 58 520
INNER ARTIFICIAL
(SNAPPER – PRODUCTIVE EARLY SEASON MARK. WATER DEPTH 12M, BEST AT NIGHT)
S 38 03 090
E 145 04 630
PATTERSON LAKES BOAT RAMP
S 38 04 437
E 145 06 968
CARRUM No1
(SNAPPER – ALL SEASON MARK. WATER DEPTH 18M)
S 38 04 478
E 145 02 126
CARRUM OUTER ARTIFICIAL
(SNAPPER)
S 38 04 800
E 145 02 100
COD HOLE
(SNAPPER)
S 38 05 866
E 145 03 539
PLANE WRECK
S 38 06 091
E 145 00 627
ASPENDALE—REC REEF
(ARTIFICIAL REEF)
S 38 02 167
E 145 04 615
SEAFORD—TEDESCO REEF
(ARTIFICIAL REEF)
S 38 05 246
E 145 05 954

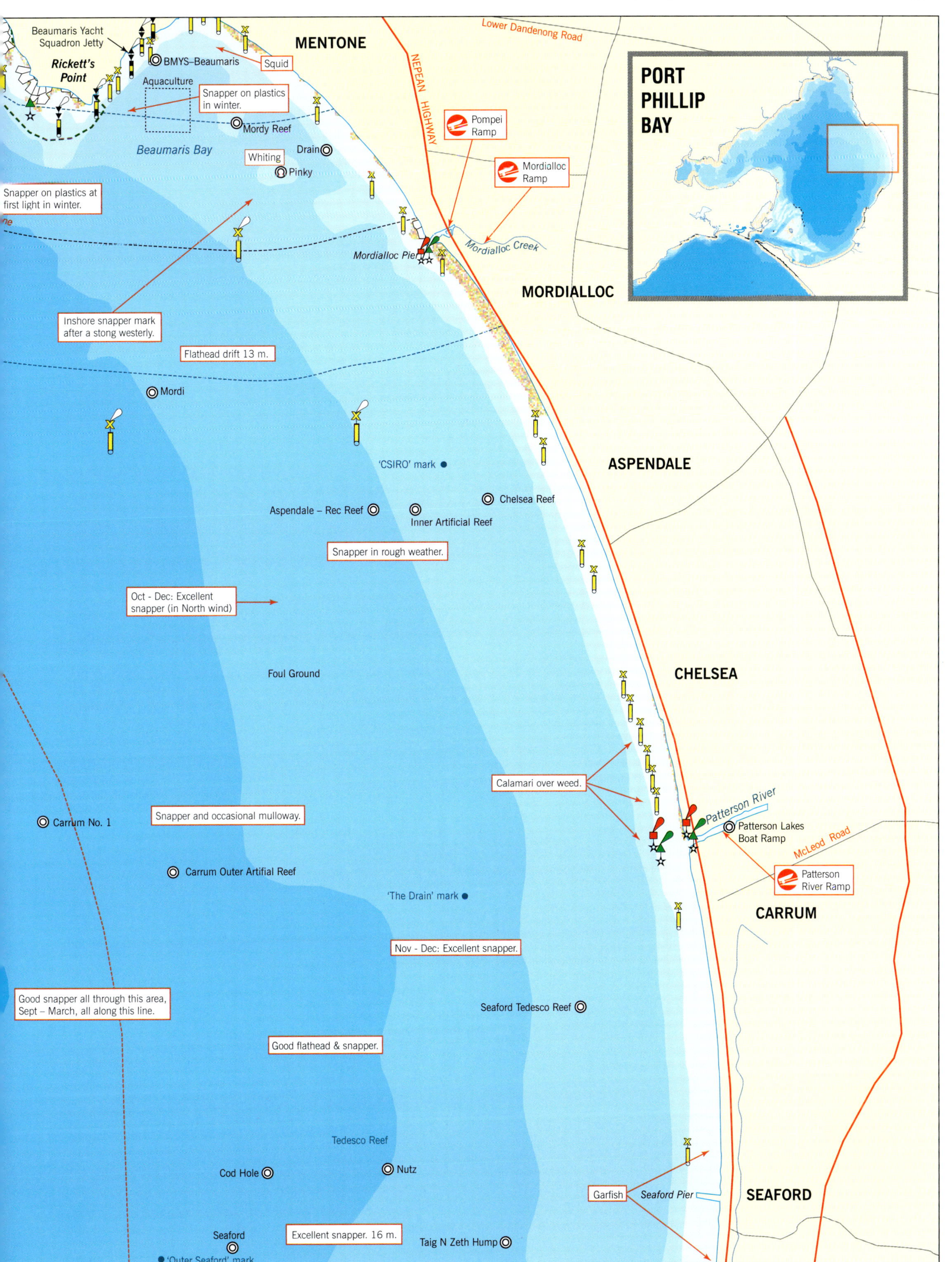

PORT PHILLIP BAY
Beaumaris Yacht Squadron Jetty
Rickett's Point
BMYS–Beaumaris
Squid
MENTONE
Lower Dandenong Road
NEPEAN HIGHWAY
Aquaculture
Snapper on plastics in winter.
Mordy Reef
Pompei Ramp
Mordialloc Ramp
Beaumaris Bay
Whiting
Drain
Pinky
Snapper on plastics at first light in winter.
Mordialloc Pier
Mordialloc Creek
MORDIALLOC
Inshore snapper mark after a stong westerly.
Flathead drift 13 m.
Mordi
'CSIRO' mark
ASPENDALE
Chelsea Reef
Aspendale – Rec Reef
Inner Artificial Reef
Snapper in rough weather.
Oct - Dec: Excellent snapper (in North wind)
Foul Ground
CHELSEA
Calamari over weed.
Patterson River
Patterson Lakes Boat Ramp
Carrum No. 1
Snapper and occasional mulloway.
McLeod Road
Patterson River Ramp
Carrum Outer Artifial Reef
'The Drain' mark
CARRUM
Nov - Dec: Excellent snapper.
Good snapper all through this area, Sept – March, all along this line.
Seaford Tedesco Reef
Good flathead & snapper.
Tedesco Reef
Cod Hole
Nutz
Garfish
Seaford Pier
SEAFORD
Seaford
Excellent snapper. 16 m.
Taig N Zeth Hump
'Outer Seaford' mark

Liddesdale Avenue. The dual launching ramp falls into relatively deep water with a safe holding jetty. Reasonable parking is available on most days, but during the summer on a hot weekend, it can be very congested.

The ramp is not suitable when heavy seas prevail from the north or west, the ideal conditions occur from the south or the east. Good snapper grounds can be reached within 5 minutes motoring from the ramp.

SHORE BASED FISHING

Patterson River

Land-Based fishing inside Patterson River is productive for a wide range of species. Fishing from the mouth rock walls in rough weather will see good catches of salmon caught when casting small metal slugs. After heavy rain, bream school up under the highway bridge and are caught on freshwater yabbies and earthworms cast unweighted to the pylons.

Throughout the winter months, anglers flicking soft plastics, metal vibes and 70 mm to 100 mm shallow diving had body lures from the mouth to the first flood gate can catch some very impressive mulloway. Most of these are caught leading up to a full moon.

Estuary perch are also an option but tend to be caught as a bi-catch on soft plastics and hard body lures fished around structure.

Fishing further up the system along the boardwalks, yellow-eye mullet are a common catch throughout the year. Dough baits seem to be the best baits.

Seaford Pier

While not a red hot location to catch fish, this pier does turn on some good garfish from time to time. Anglers in search of garfish should concentrate heavily throughout September and October when the larger models are available. Berley is essential with a float setup best offered. Casting a paternoster rig as far as you can will see some goof flathead taken. The last few seasons have also seen some snapper taken during rough weather by anglers happy to brave the conditions.

In the general area from the Patterson River mouth to Frankston, there are also some decent flounder and plenty of sand crabs for those who like the wade the shallows looking for them.

Even if you don't have your own boat, fishing on a local fishing charter can be a lot of fun.

Frankston Pier

Every year this easily accessible spot produces more fish and better fish. However it is best known for the great numbers of garfish that can be taken from the pier for most of the year. Casting baits into deeper water also sees you in with a chance of good flathead, salmon and snapper.

One of the real attractions of the pier these days are the salmon that come into the shallow water and gutter that can be found about half way along the pier during strong south and south-west winds. Fishing here with a bit of berley and either paternoster style rigs or even a lightly weighted pilchard, will produce some great fishing for salmon up to 3 kg and more. Anglers also throw lures, especially soft plastics, around the pier and have great success on the salmon and pinky snapper.

During strong a southerly blow, the water becomes stirred up and attracts plenty of salmon and pinkie snapper toward the pier. At the third flag pole from the beginning of the pier, a shallow gutter runs both south to Olivers Hill and north to Paterson River. Berleying with mashed up pilchards can see some nice sized pinkie snapper caught during strong southerly and westerly winds. Unweighted strips of pilchard fillet work extremely well on light tackle.

During summer it is worth catching a garfish and putting it out live under a float, as rat kingfish often frequent the pier and come racing through upsetting the gars.

Back towards the creek there are usually mullet to be found and a little berley over the shallows will bring them in if they are nearby.

At times, there has been the odd trevally caught close into the pylons on sandworms, however the worms usually seem to attract unwanted fish like cobblers (gurnard family) and toadfish. There's good fun for the junior anglers on a summer evening just before dusk when the flathead and small snapper become active near the end of the pier.

For years the experienced garfish anglers have headed for the pier on a northerly. Northerlies take the floats over the weed beds on the Olivers Hill side of the pier and some top catches are taken here. When the creek is dirty, a flood tide keeps the discoloured water away from this better garfish spot.

Kananook Creek

Rarely fished, the Kananook Creek abounds with bream. Land-Based fishing is the only option and most anglers have success with unweighted prawns and mussel cast along the edges of the creek. The creek is quite dirty but there are plenty of bream on offer along the edges if you're prepared to walk.

After heavy rain, bream tend to gather at the boat ramp and mouth and can be caught using freshwater yabbies and earthworms.

Olivers Hill Rocks

There are some suitable rocks for fishing towards Olivers Hill from the boat ramp at the intersection of Liddesdale Avenue and the Nepean Highway.

Fishing with bait on the bottom here is tough on tackle and while there are wrasse and leather jacket to be caught, the best results come from those anglers who take a light rod and cast squid jigs around the reefy areas, especially on the high tide as the squid move into the shallows to feed. Garfish are plentiful in the area year round. Best success is when you anchor adjacent to the reefs and berley with bran and tuna oil. A small float setup works well with silverfish a top bait.

CHAPTER 9
FRANKSTON TO MOUNT MARTHA
MAPS 12 & 13

This area lacks suitable places to launch boats but it is a very productive area nonetheless. Shore anglers have access to arguably the two best shore spots in the bay, being Mornington Pier and the Bradford Road rock platform at Mount Martha.

North winds can cause huge seas in this area. Easterlies seem to flatten the sea but this wind is not recognised as being ideal for snapper fishing close inshore. (This is despite the fact that some of the deepest parts of the Bay are within only 1 km of the shore here.) Best snapper breeze is west to south-west and possibly south. Early in a northerly there are fish taken but the problem of retrieving a boat in very lumpy seas is a deterrent to most anglers.

Sand and weed patches are prevalent through this part of the bay. A good spot to try for whiting, red mullet, flathead and trevally is the area of weed and reef about 200 m out from Sunnyside Beach.

There are reefs around Daveys Bay, off Canadian Bay and also at `Cahills', a locally known reef north of Graces Jetty at Junyung Road. Good pinkys are taken here.

There is a reef area right through to Dromana, but it comes to a sudden end when the drop-off to the rubble occurs, usually about 200 to 300 m out from the shore. Usually the snapper appear late August or early September and carry on through to the next season.

Flathead in the area are small and usually a menace to snapper anglers. Gars are prolific and while on the small side, they appear to be around most of the year, although they are quiet when the first cold snap comes. Pinkys appear after Christmas and the whiting, while not fished for by many anglers, appear in the spring and disappear, probably into the deeper waters, in autumn.

BOAT FISHING – WHERE TO FISH

Hospital

If you listen to the marine radio chatter in this area you will hear the hospital referred to often. It is the geriatric hospital at Mount Eliza. Directly off-shore from this hospital are some prime snapper grounds where the depth of 16 to 18 m is very productive. The advantage of the deep water is that the fish are likely to bite during the day. At the change of tide mid afternoon and then fishing to dark is the best.

Pier fishing around the Bay can lead to catches of many different species.

Ansetts

The famous Ansett residence and property is well known to anglers in the area as many good catches of snapper are taken out from here. Neil Thompson, has generously given his mark off Ansetts where he has had tremendous success in November and December and then again in April and May. Looking towards the shore from about 3 km out, you will notice a green water tower on top of the hill behind Ansetts. The main residence at Ansetts lines up with the tower.

Then, looking south towards Arthurs Seat at Dromana, the television relay towers will line up with the right hand point of Martha Point before it hits the water. You are in snapper territory here with mud, rubble and scallops and about 19 m of water under the boat.

Pier Mark (Mornington)

Due west of the Mornington Pier and about 3 km out, there is a very productive area with a similar bottom to Ansetts where professional fishermen long-line medium size snapper. Many fish have been caught here in the 2 to 3 kg class so perhaps a smaller bait is worth a try. Half a garfish on a gang of three hooks is sometimes the answer to the faster biting smaller snapper.

Looking back to the pier, a prominent red brick house will just cut the corner of the Melbourne end of the pier. The other line is the same as for Ansetts looking towards Arthurs Seat. Usually there is a red yachting buoy located in this general area. Some nice size flathead have been found here. While waiting for snapper, use a silver wobbler or a Mister Twister on a light garfish rod, lower the lure to the bottom and lift it about a metre off the seabed. Then raise the lure slowly and allow it to fall. Several large flathead can mill around the lure and if it is your day, you can get half a dozen nice size 'frogs'.

The Poplars

About 400 to 500 m off Bird Rock, located directly below the Mount Martha Motel on the Esplanade, there is a very productive area of reef. Amongst this reef there are odd holes that carry whiting, pinky snapper, red mullet, leatherjacket, trevally and some very nice sized flathead. This is a reliable mark where Neil Thomson has enjoyed success on whiting after a session in the deeper water chasing snapper.

The Ski Jump

Out about the same distance as the Mount Martha cliff, looking south towards Dromana, this is a very productive heavy reef area where most species are taken, including some big snapper when the seas are fairly rough. A good line is looking directly up the street to the right of the Mount Martha Store which can be seen from this point. You look straight up the street and have the poles in line. Locals liken it to looking right up the slope of a ski jump.

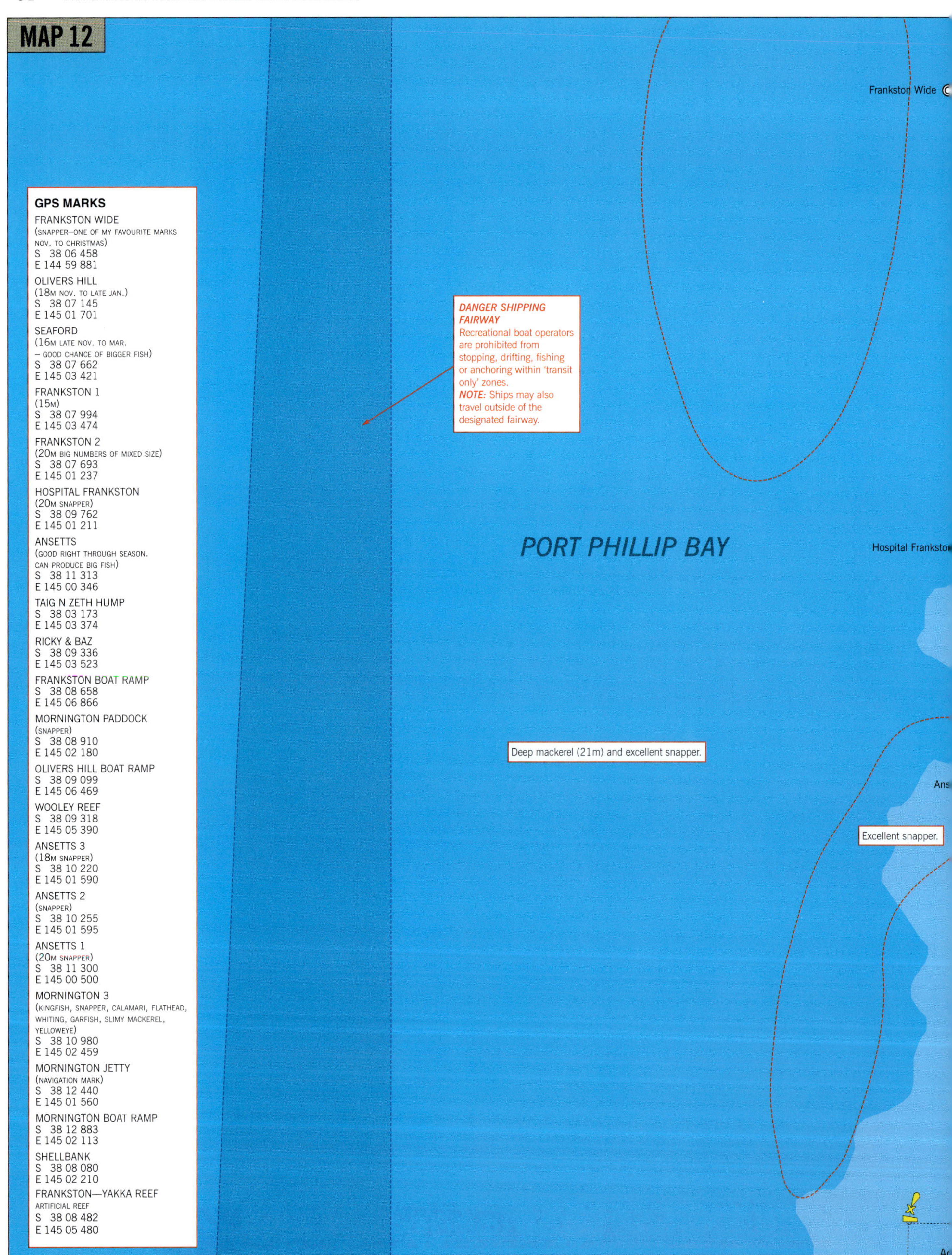
MAP 12
GPS MARKS
FRANKSTON WIDE
(SNAPPER—ONE OF MY FAVOURITE MARKS NOV. TO CHRISTMAS)
S 38 06 458
E 144 59 881
OLIVERS HILL
(18M NOV. TO LATE JAN.)
S 38 07 145
E 145 01 701
SEAFORD
(16M LATE NOV. TO MAR. – GOOD CHANCE OF BIGGER FISH)
S 38 07 662
E 145 03 421
FRANKSTON 1
(15M)
S 38 07 994
E 145 03 474
FRANKSTON 2
(20M BIG NUMBERS OF MIXED SIZE)
S 38 07 693
E 145 01 237
HOSPITAL FRANKSTON
(20M SNAPPER)
S 38 09 762
E 145 01 211
ANSETTS
(GOOD RIGHT THROUGH SEASON. CAN PRODUCE BIG FISH)
S 38 11 313
E 145 00 346
TAIG N ZETH HUMP
S 38 03 173
E 145 03 374
RICKY & BAZ
S 38 09 336
E 145 03 523
FRANKSTON BOAT RAMP
S 38 08 658
E 145 06 866
MORNINGTON PADDOCK
(SNAPPER)
S 38 08 910
E 145 02 180
OLIVERS HILL BOAT RAMP
S 38 09 099
E 145 06 469
WOOLEY REEF
S 38 09 318
E 145 05 390
ANSETTS 3
(18M SNAPPER)
S 38 10 220
E 145 01 590
ANSETTS 2
(SNAPPER)
S 38 10 255
E 145 01 595
ANSETTS 1
(20M SNAPPER)
S 38 11 300
E 145 00 500
MORNINGTON 3
(KINGFISH, SNAPPER, CALAMARI, FLATHEAD, WHITING, GARFISH, SLIMY MACKEREL, YELLOWEYE)
S 38 10 980
E 145 02 459
MORNINGTON JETTY
(NAVIGATION MARK)
S 38 12 440
E 145 01 560
MORNINGTON BOAT RAMP
S 38 12 883
E 145 02 113
SHELLBANK
S 38 08 080
E 145 02 210
FRANKSTON—YAKKA REEF
ARTIFICIAL REEF
S 38 08 482
E 145 05 480
DANGER SHIPPING FAIRWAY
Recreational boat operators are prohibited from stopping, drifting, fishing or anchoring within 'transit only' zones.
NOTE: Ships may also travel outside of the designated fairway.
Frankston Wide
PORT PHILLIP BAY
Hospital Frankston
Deep mackerel (21m) and excellent snapper.
Excellent snapper.

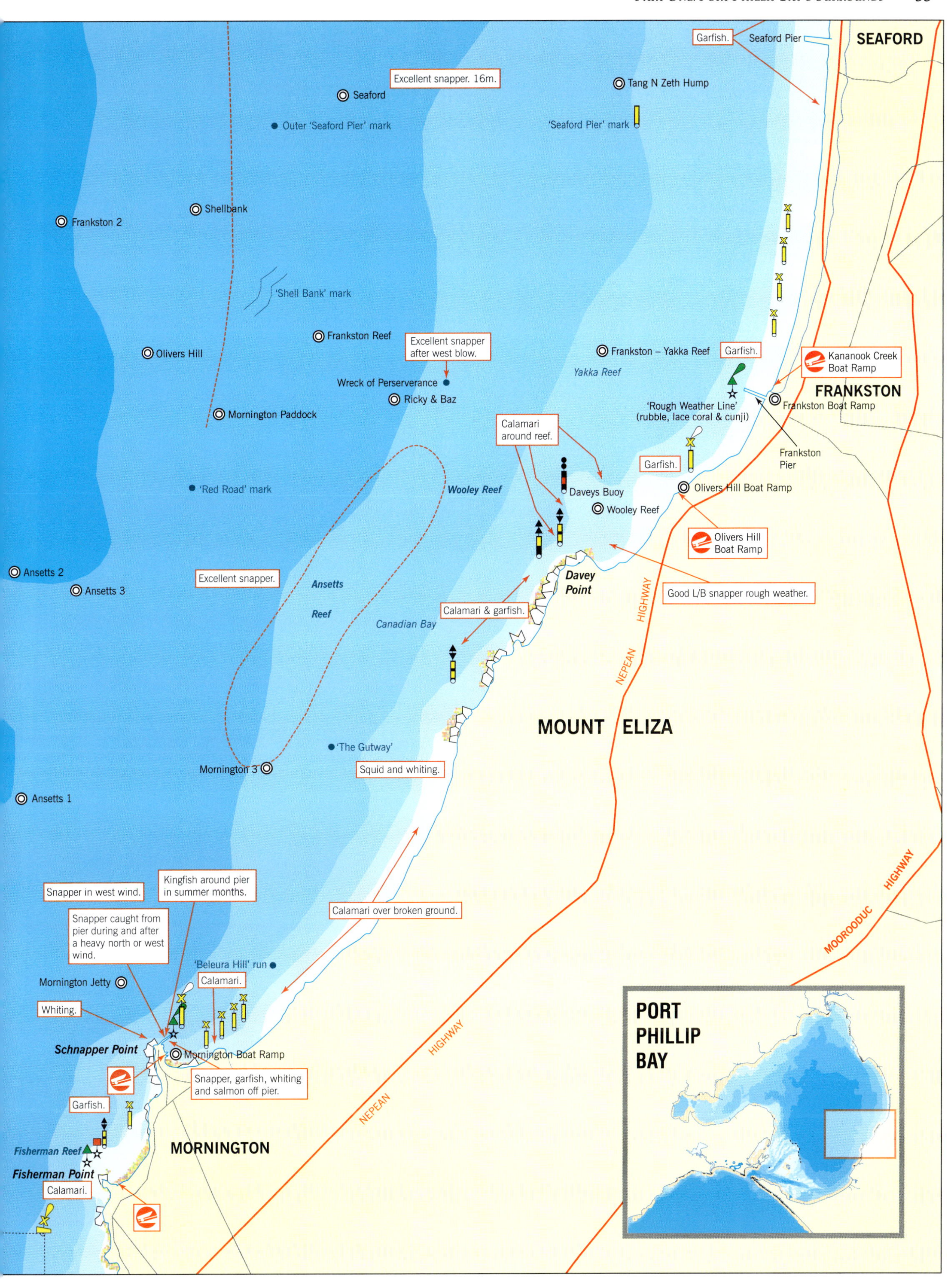
Garfish.
Seaford Pier
SEAFORD
Excellent snapper. 16m.
Seaford
Tang N Zeth Hump
Outer 'Seaford Pier' mark
'Seaford Pier' mark
Shellbank
Frankston 2
'Shell Bank' mark
Frankston Reef
Excellent snapper after west blow.
Olivers Hill
Frankston – Yakka Reef
Garfish.
Kananook Creek Boat Ramp
Yakka Reef
FRANKSTON
Wreck of Perserverance
Ricky & Baz
Mornington Paddock
'Rough Weather Line' (rubble, lace coral & cunji)
Frankston Boat Ramp
Calamari around reef.
Frankston Pier
Garfish.
Olivers Hill Boat Ramp
'Red Road' mark
Wooley Reef
Daveys Buoy
Wooley Reef
Olivers Hill Boat Ramp
Ansetts 2
Ansetts 3
Excellent snapper.
Ansetts
Reef
Davey Point
HIGHWAY
Good L/B snapper rough weather.
Calamari & garfish.
Canadian Bay
NEPEAN
MOUNT ELIZA
'The Gutway'
Mornington 3
Squid and whiting.
Ansetts 1
Kingfish around pier in summer months.
Snapper in west wind.
Snapper caught from pier during and after a heavy north or west wind.
Calamari over broken ground.
HIGHWAY
MOOROODUC
'Beleura Hill' run
Mornington Jetty
Calamari.
Whiting.
Schnapper Point
Mornington Boat Ramp
HIGHWAY
Snapper, garfish, whiting and salmon off pier.
Garfish.
NEPEAN
Fisherman Reef
MORNINGTON
Fisherman Point
Calamari.
PORT PHILLIP BAY

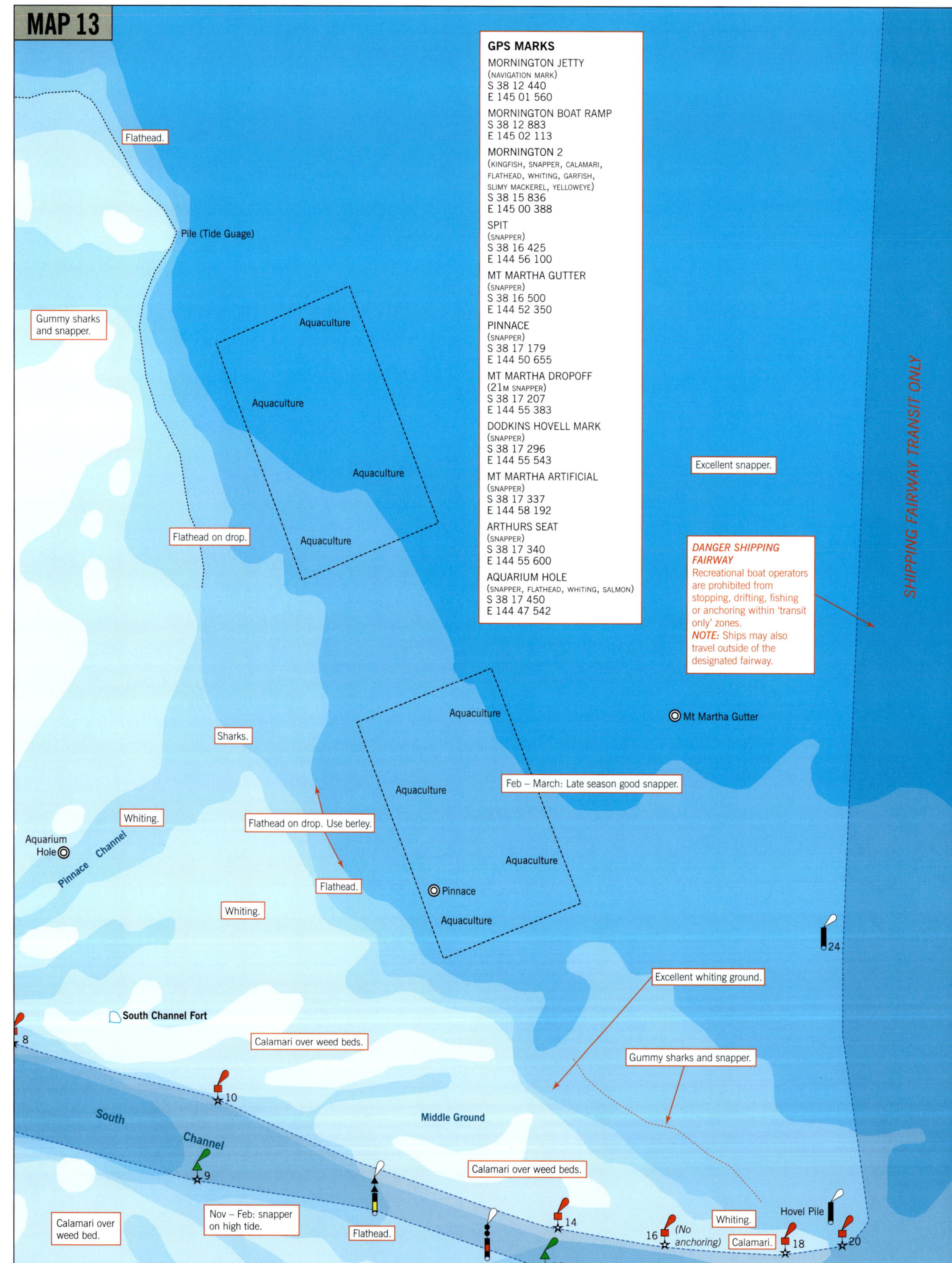
MAP 13
GPS MARKS
MORNINGTON JETTY
(NAVIGATION MARK)
S 38 12 440
E 145 01 560
MORNINGTON BOAT RAMP
S 38 12 883
E 145 02 113
MORNINGTON 2
(KINGFISH, SNAPPER, CALAMARI, FLATHEAD, WHITING, GARFISH, SLIMY MACKEREL, YELLOWEYE)
S 38 15 836
E 145 00 388
SPIT
(SNAPPER)
S 38 16 425
E 144 56 100
MT MARTHA GUTTER
(SNAPPER)
S 38 16 500
E 144 52 350
PINNACE
(SNAPPER)
S 38 17 179
E 144 50 655
MT MARTHA DROPOFF
(21M SNAPPER)
S 38 17 207
E 144 55 383
DODKINS HOVELL MARK
(SNAPPER)
S 38 17 296
E 144 55 543
MT MARTHA ARTIFICIAL
(SNAPPER)
S 38 17 337
E 144 58 192
ARTHURS SEAT
(SNAPPER)
S 38 17 340
E 144 55 600
AQUARIUM HOLE
(SNAPPER, FLATHEAD, WHITING, SALMON)
S 38 17 450
E 144 47 542
Flathead.
Pile (Tide Guage)
Gummy sharks and snapper.
Aquaculture
Aquaculture
Aquaculture
Aquaculture
Flathead on drop.
Excellent snapper.
SHIPPING FAIRWAY TRANSIT ONLY
DANGER SHIPPING FAIRWAY
Recreational boat operators are prohibited from stopping, drifting, fishing or anchoring within 'transit only' zones.
NOTE: Ships may also travel outside of the designated fairway.
Aquaculture
Mt Martha Gutter
Sharks.
Aquaculture
Feb – March: Late season good snapper.
Whiting.
Flathead on drop. Use berley.
Aquarium Hole
Pinnace Channel
Aquaculture
Flathead.
Pinnace
Whiting.
Aquaculture
24
Excellent whiting ground.
South Channel Fort
8
Calamari over weed beds.
Gummy sharks and snapper.
10
South Channel
Middle Ground
9
Calamari over weed beds.
Calamari over weed bed.
Nov – Feb: snapper on high tide.
Flathead.
14
16
(No anchoring)
Whiting.
Calamari.
Hovel Pile
18
20

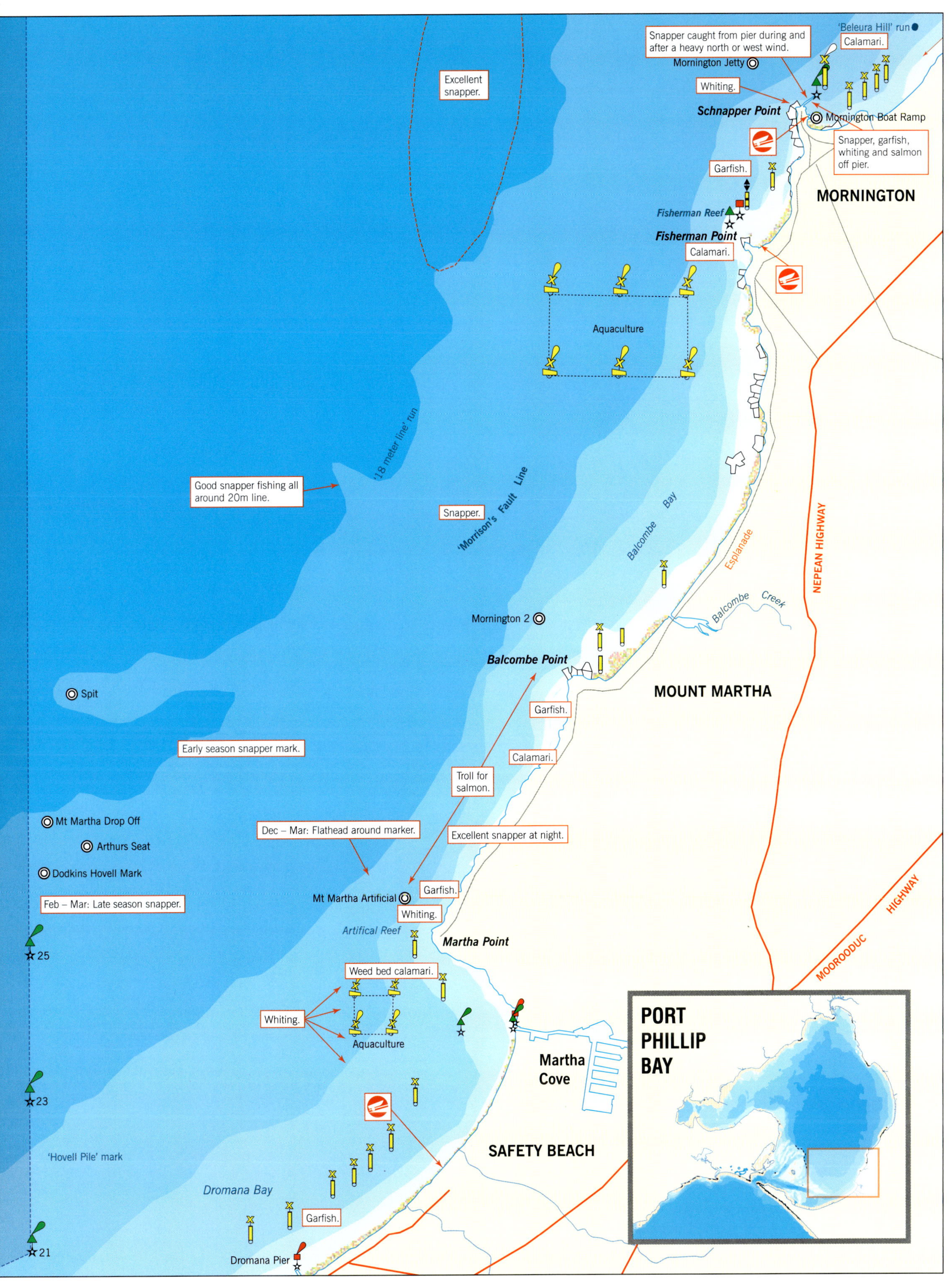

'Beleura Hill' run
Calamari.
Snapper caught from pier during and after a heavy north or west wind.
Mornington Jetty
Whiting.
Schnapper Point
Mornington Boat Ramp
Snapper, garfish, whiting and salmon off pier.
Excellent snapper.
Garfish.
MORNINGTON
Fisherman Reef
Fisherman Point
Calamari.
Aquaculture
'18 meter line' run
Good snapper fishing all around 20m line.
Snapper.
'Morrison's Fault Line
Balcombe Bay
Esplanade
NEPEAN HIGHWAY
Balcombe Creek
Mornington 2
Balcombe Point
MOUNT MARTHA
Spit
Garfish.
Early season snapper mark.
Calamari.
Troll for salmon.
Mt Martha Drop Off
Arthurs Seat
Dec – Mar: Flathead around marker.
Excellent snapper at night.
Dodkins Hovell Mark
Mt Martha Artificial
Garfish.
Feb – Mar: Late season snapper.
Whiting.
Artifical Reef
Martha Point
25
Weed bed calamari.
MOOROODUC HIGHWAY
Whiting.
Aquaculture
Martha Cove
PORT PHILLIP BAY
23
SAFETY BEACH
'Hovell Pile' mark
Dromana Bay
Garfish.
21
Dromana Pier

Mitch Bertacchini from Online Fishing Charters understands how important it is to use his fish finder in order to regularly find schools of snapper in the bay.

Good whiting, pinkys, gars and trevally are caught here from November through to March.

Caution: Because Sunnyside Beach is a free bathing beach it always attracts boating traffic. Heavy reef exists very close to shore here and several boats have been holed over the years.

When going to sea from the main Mornington boat ramp, watch out for moorings unmarked by buoys. Sometimes they can become entangled in propellers and spoil a days outing. Heavy reef is also marked by pylons at Fishermens Beach and further south at Bird Rock, where it is wise to keep at least 200 m out from the main platform.

Martha Deep

During a run in tide, snapper move out of the shipping channel and begin to explore the flat sandy bottom. The area is around 21 meters deep and is prolific with snapper late in the season during February and March. As funny as it sounds, the best snapper fishing occurs when a ship passes by. It is said that the ships propellers stir up the bottom, hence they come on the bite. The window is short but is productive.

GPS Co-ordinates
S 38 14.339
E 144 55.428

BOAT RAMPS

Mornington: The Schnapper Point boat ramp is an excellent dual lane ramp protected in most weather except strong northerlies.

Fishermens Beach Boat Ramp: This dual ramp is located on the Esplanade at Mornington, just south of Webb Street. The facilities here are second rate, the ramp is shallow, it has dangerous reef all around it and if you are not in the first dozen to the ramp, parking becomes a problem. The ideal launching conditions here are southerlies and easterlies.

SHORE BASED FISHING

Mornington Pier

A decent cast off the end of this pier will see your bait in 8 m or more of water which is part of the reason it fishes so well. In fact, this is a top place to fish for snapper during rough weather from the south-west in October, November and December, and at these times it is often shoulder to shoulder with anglers.

The pier tends to produce most of the species on offer in the bay depending on time of year, but generally speaking it features an excellent population of squid almost all year, as well as garfish and flathead. Besides these regular species, other common catches include salmon and barracouta, which can be taken on lures or with a pilchard under a float.

The winter months see good numbers of pinky snapper, and as mentioned above, larger fish in season. However the real excitement over the past few summers has been good numbers of kingfish hanging around the pier, busting off unsuspecting anglers and putting up a great battle for those who target them.

This pier is widely recognised in the top bracket of piers around the bay, and it's a place that can produce all day long and all year. Specifically, the deep water at the end produces something for the patient angler. Then from halfway out to the very end of the pier, flathead can be taken at most times of the year when smooth seas prevail.

Big snapper come very close to shore near the rocky breakwall in big seas caused by west and south-westerly winds—it is generally thought that unless the waves are breaking over the pier it is not suitable for snapper fishing.

Barracouta have disappeared somewhat over the last few years but a few small ones can still be taken on lures fishing on the lee of the pier.

The smaller holding jetties in the harbour fish well for leatherjacket, red mullet, the occasional whiting and the ever-hungry parrot fish which provide good sport for junior anglers.

Rocks—Mornington to Mount Martha

There are several good rock platforms to fish from in this area. Best conditions are when the wind is in the south quarter. Quality flathead, garfish and leatherjackets have been caught, but if trying for snapper, stingrays and banjo sharks can be a problem.

Surf casting gear is essential to reach the deep water but light tackle can be used to fish around the rocks. Berley is an advantage if allowed to wash against the rocks and distribute. The main target species in these locations are squid and garfish, both of which are common.

Bradford Road

As the name suggests, this rock ledge lies at the bottom of Bradford Road at Mount Martha. This spot drops into deep water almost at your feet and produces some very good snapper fishing for those anglers who put in the time and effort. The ledge also produces salmon and plenty of squid and garfish. Garfish are prolific and are caught using a float setup. Berley is the key and the gars can be of exceptional size during September.

Frankston Pier is a popular structure for anglers to sit and target garfish throughout the year.

CHAPTER 10
MOUNT MARTHA TO PORTSEA (Including Mud Island)
MAPS 13, 14 & 15

Port Phillip Bay takes on a different make-up here. If you draw a straight line between Dromana and Werribee, the bay to the south becomes a very fast flowing tidal area similar to most parts of Western Port.

This area is a mixture of sandbanks, channels and relatively shallow areas formed by the huge volume of water travelling through on the tide.

A lot of fishing is done east of the sandy areas that run between Mud Island and the Hovell Pile. The channels that run either side of the shallows hold good numbers of sharks, snapper, whiting and big flathead.

One problem that anglers have here is working out the flow of the tide. The flow of water often traps inexperienced people. While the gazetted tide change is correct, the actual flow continues about 3 hours after `the change'. This delay is due to the volume of water either in the held in the bay on a run out tide, or the build up of water outside the `Rip' on a flood tide. If anglers take the gazetted tide change at Williamstown (which is 3 hours after Port Phillip Heads) they will be pretty right for the flow changes.

Like Western Port, the flow of water makes a difference to the catches. The shallow areas are better for sharks and snapper.

For some reason various areas fish better on certain tides. For instance, there is better fishing from Sorrento to Portsea on the ebb (run-out) tide. On the other hand, the flood tide is better for working the channels around Mud Island, and from Blairgowrie to Rye.

Overall this is a very productive part of the bay for fishing, but it takes some working out. The area has some productive piers and is well served with good launching facilities at Rye and Sorrento.

BOAT FISHING – WHERE TO FISH

Hovell Pile

This pile marks the end of the Middle Grounds, where large ships using the South Shipping Channel turn and make their way to the Port of Melbourne. The water is very deep around the pile and once again it has predominantly a scallop and mussel bottom. There have been good hauls of snapper 300 m due west of the Hovell Pile.

Anglers fishing this area should be aware of all shipping and boating activity and should keep out of the shipping lanes to prevent being fined (or worse!)

To the east of the Hovell Pile, the bank rises to around five meters deep. The bottom is scatted with seaweed growth making it an inviting location to catch calamari. Whiting are also about and greater in numbers by February and March.

Middle Ground

This area is subject to massive sand shifts that can alter the makeup of the sea floor from year to year. However, there are some excellent weed and sand patch areas here that will hold good numbers of King George whiting, red mullet, trevally and some thumping big `yank' flathead.

It is best to fish the flood tide (same tide time as Williamstown) and anchor away from the fishing area. Then use long casts with light sinkers into the sand holes. At times, leatherjacket around 10 cm in length are in plague proportions. Berleying close to the boat can attract all unwanted fish close to the stern, so fish well behind the boat for the targeted fish. Garfish will also move in on berley trail and while the 'un-wanteds' are around, fishing a float setup just out the back can lead to some very healthy nags of gars.

South Channel Fort

This is simply a rocky island in the middle of the Bay. It is located north of the South Channel. The Pinnace Channel runs between it and Mud Island to the west. The area around the Fort is a series of weed and sand holes, with open patches of sand and shell dropping off into deeper channels. At times late in the season (March to May) good catches of King George whiting are taken right up against the island itself. It is best to anchor in about 3 to 4 m of water and then cast into water about 1.5 to 2 m in depth. The whiting caught here have been quite large, although early in the season (pre Christmas) there have been several good bags of fish 30 cm in length.

The drop-offs also offer a good chance of a big flathead. Anchor with the tide and allow a berley trail to work its way into the channel. You will find that the big flatties will soon get a whiff of the action and turn up. The best time to do this is late in the ebb tide (change of tide).

Capel Sound

This area is very deep and popular with locals for snapper and gummy sharks. The best time to fish here for snapper is September to December and then again around Easter. On a good day you can see clearly to the bottom of the channel edge. Big whiting are taken here on the last of the ebb tide and the first of the flood. Due to the surrounding banks being quite shallow, working soft plastics lures along the drop-off is a productive technique for flathead. During the last of the flood tides, flathead will perch on the edges of the drop awaiting an easy meal.

Caution: Anglers are reminded that it is an offence against Port Rule 62A to anchor in the shipping channels between the Heads and the Hovell Pile on the South Channel side of the Bay, and also between the Heads and the West Channel Pile on the West Channel side of the Bay. The wake formed by passing ships can also be hazardous to the unwary angler.

South Sand

This sand patch is a huge expanse of ground that offers a wide variety of fishing opportunities. Good catches of calamari squid are taken here by anglers drifting over the broken ground. This ground comprises weed, mussels and sand patches with huge areas of open sand. There are also some terrific flathead to be taken here and one very good method is to drift with pilchards.

Large numbers of whiting also move over this area in summer and they can be caught in bag limit numbers in spring and again late in the season around Easter.

Channel Marker No.10

Along the shallows of Channel Marker No.10 there is plenty of calamari to be caught. This location isn't fished by many but does produce plenty of smaller size calamari year round. Fishing during the early morning on a high tide is the most productive time. Drifting over the weed beds is the best technique. Try using smaller sized jigs in the 2.0-2.5 size for best results.

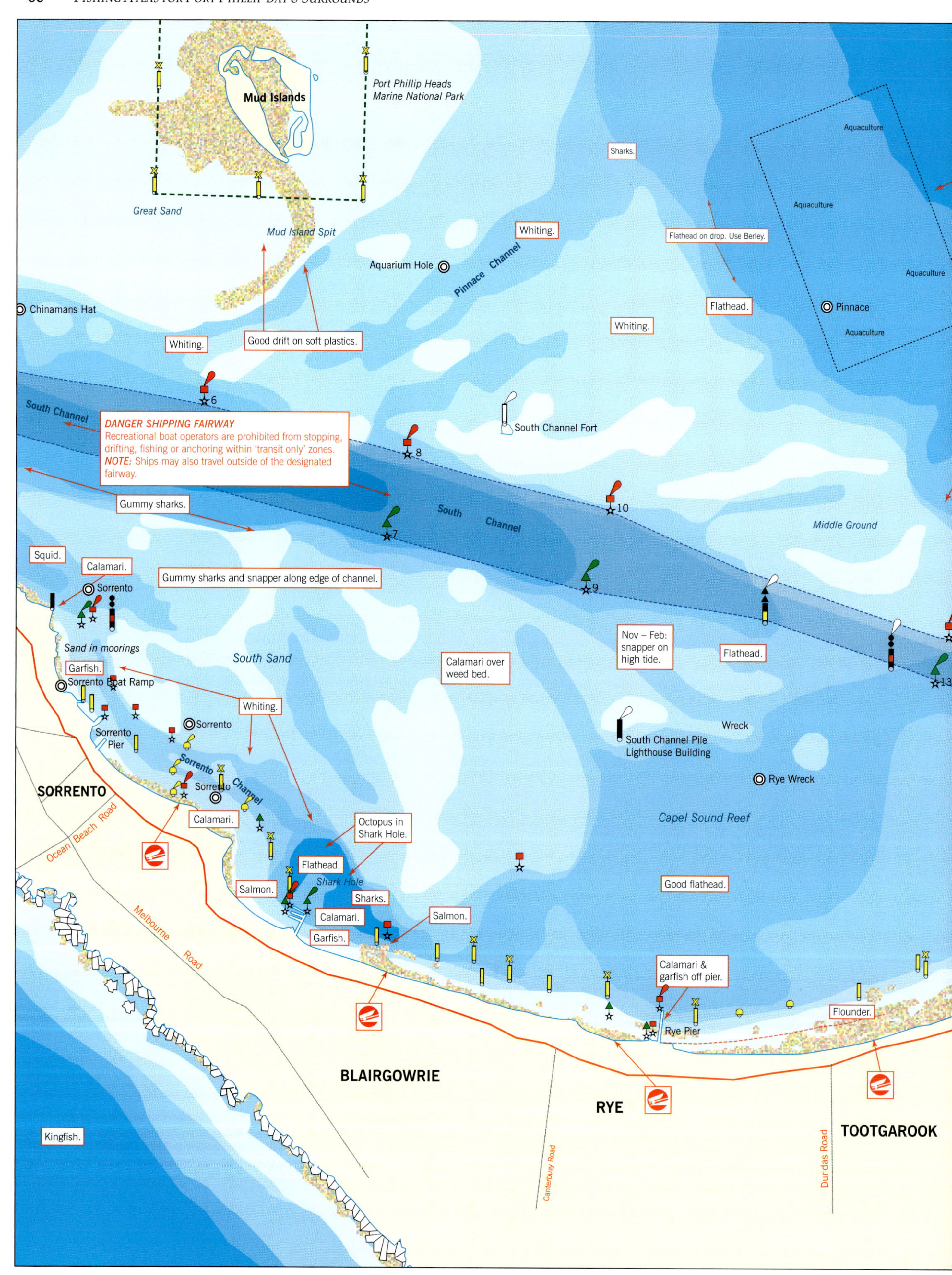

Mud Islands
Port Phillip Heads
Marine National Park
Great Sand
Mud Island Spit
Sharks.
Aquaculture
Aquaculture
Aquaculture
Aquaculture
Whiting.
Flathead on drop. Use Berley.
Aquarium Hole
Pinnace Channel
Chinamans Hat
Flathead.
Pinnace
Whiting.
Whiting.
Good drift on soft plastics.
6
South Channel
South Channel Fort
DANGER SHIPPING FAIRWAY
Recreational boat operators are prohibited from stopping, drifting, fishing or anchoring within 'transit only' zones.
NOTE: Ships may also travel outside of the designated fairway.
8
10
Gummy sharks.
South Channel
7
Middle Ground
Squid.
Calamari.
Gummy sharks and snapper along edge of channel.
Sorrento
9
Nov – Feb: snapper on high tide.
Sand in moorings
South Sand
Calamari over weed bed.
Flathead.
Garfish.
Sorrento Boat Ramp
13
Whiting.
Wreck
Sorrento
Sorrento Pier
South Channel Pile Lighthouse Building
Sorrento Channel
SORRENTO
Sorrento
Rye Wreck
Calamari.
Ocean Beach Road
Octopus in Shark Hole.
Capel Sound Reef
Flathead.
Shark Hole
Salmon.
Good flathead.
Sharks.
Calamari.
Salmon.
Garfish.
Melbourne Road
Calamari & garfish off pier.
Flounder.
Rye Pier
BLAIRGOWRIE
RYE
TOOTGAROOK
Kingfish.
Canterbury Road
Durdas Road

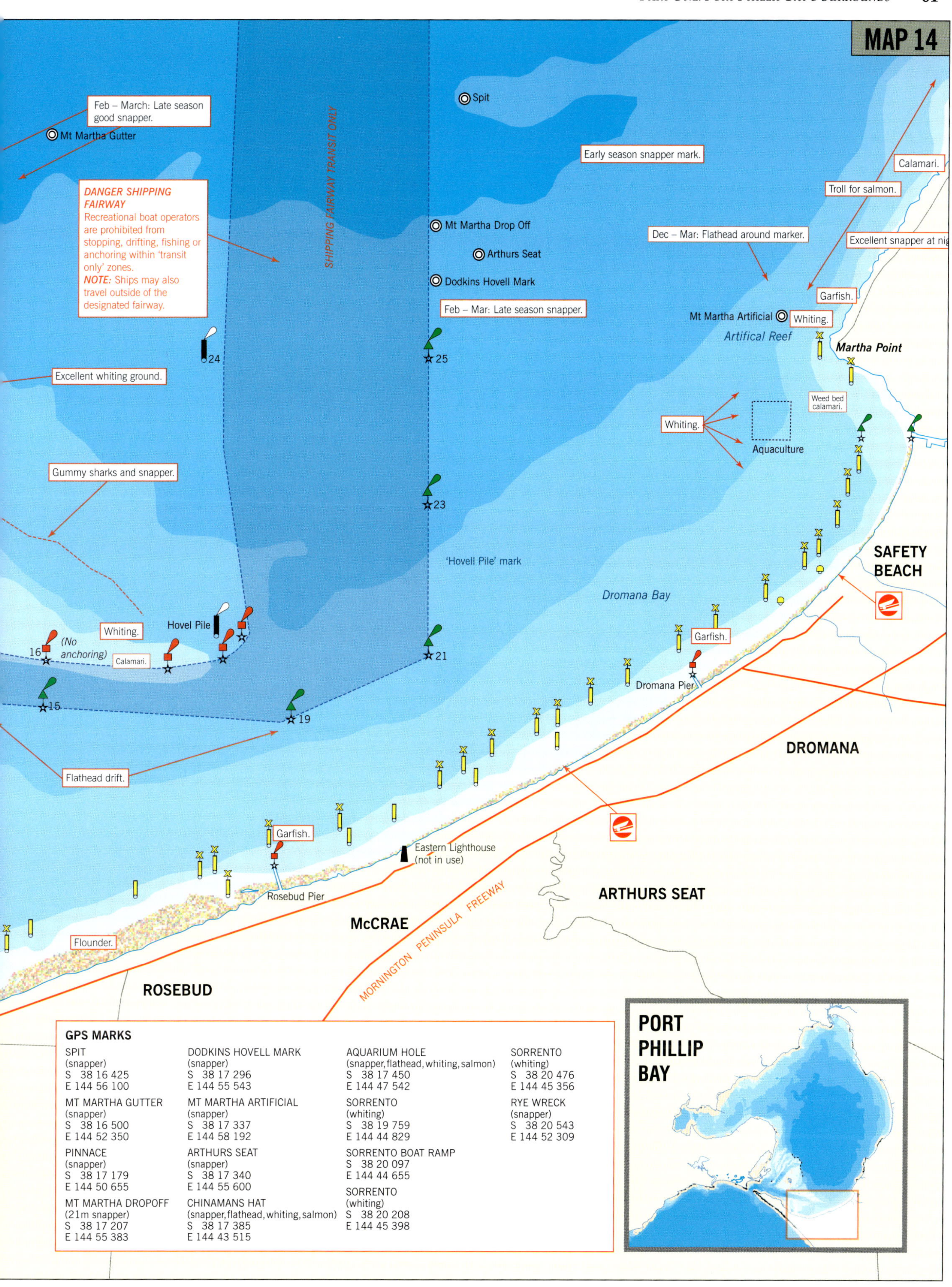
MAP 14
Spit
Feb – March: Late season good snapper.
Mt Martha Gutter
Early season snapper mark.
Calamari.
Troll for salmon.
DANGER SHIPPING FAIRWAY
Recreational boat operators are prohibited from stopping, drifting, fishing or anchoring within 'transit only' zones.
NOTE: Ships may also travel outside of the designated fairway.
SHIPPING FAIRWAY TRANSIT ONLY
Mt Martha Drop Off
Arthurs Seat
Dodkins Hovell Mark
Dec – Mar: Flathead around marker.
Excellent snapper at
Feb – Mar: Late season snapper.
Garfish.
Mt Martha Artificial
Whiting.
Artifical Reef
Martha Point
24
25
Excellent whiting ground.
Weed bed calamari.
Whiting.
Aquaculture
Gummy sharks and snapper.
23
'Hovell Pile' mark
SAFETY BEACH
Dromana Bay
Hovel Pile
Whiting.
(No anchoring)
16
Calamari.
21
Garfish.
Dromana Pier
15
19
DROMANA
Flathead drift.
Garfish.
Eastern Lighthouse (not in use)
Rosebud Pier
ARTHURS SEAT
McCRAE
MORNINGTON PENINSULA FREEWAY
Flounder.
ROSEBUD
PORT PHILLIP BAY
GPS MARKS
SPIT (snapper) S 38 16 425 E 144 56 100
MT MARTHA GUTTER (snapper) S 38 16 500 E 144 52 350
PINNACE (snapper) S 38 17 179 E 144 50 655
MT MARTHA DROPOFF (21m snapper) S 38 17 207 E 144 55 383
DODKINS HOVELL MARK (snapper) S 38 17 296 E 144 55 543
MT MARTHA ARTIFICIAL (snapper) S 38 17 337 E 144 58 192
ARTHURS SEAT (snapper) S 38 17 340 E 144 55 600
CHINAMANS HAT (snapper, flathead, whiting, salmon) S 38 17 385 E 144 43 515
AQUARIUM HOLE (snapper, flathead, whiting, salmon) S 38 17 450 E 144 47 542
SORRENTO (whiting) S 38 19 759 E 144 44 829
SORRENTO BOAT RAMP S 38 20 097 E 144 44 655
SORRENTO (whiting) S 38 20 208 E 144 45 398
SORRENTO (whiting) S 38 20 476 E 144 45 356
RYE WRECK (snapper) S 38 20 543 E 144 52 309

The south channel marker is a top location to target calamari and whiting.

South Channel Edge

This area is the drop-off to the South Channel. Once again be aware where you can anchor and where you cannot. There are some nice snapper to be taken here on the last of the ebb tide and the first of the flood. Drift until a small pinky is caught; then anchor on the edge of the drop-off and fish with heavy sinkers.

By working along the edge to find areas of reef, this is a top location to find huge gummy sharks. To catch them it takes patience and fresh baits such as trevally and salmon. Just remember these fish, which are often over 20 kg, are very old and important breeders, so it pays to let them go.

The Shark Hole

The Shark Hole is located in the Sorrento Channel between Rye and Blairgowrie, it is about 17 m deep and is clearly marked on most maps and admiralty charts of the area.

Some solid snapper have been taken in the past but it is the type of location that doesn't 'explode' with fish. Rather, providing you are patient, your catch might be only two or three fish but they will be of exceptional size.

The Sisters

These two conspicuous rocky headlands are located between Hughes Road and Collins Parade off the Nepean Highway at Sorrento. The Sorrento Channel runs very close to shore here, and anywhere between where the blue water meets the sand and the shore near The Sisters, is prime whiting ground.

Towards Rye, the channel gets deeper and the area supports good snapper. Pinkys also bite well off The Sisters especially in the summer, early morning and late evening. A trolled garfish or a Nilsmaster lure in the Sorrento Channel will often produce a few good-sized snook.

Sorrento Channel

This is a deep channel that runs between `The Sisters' and Point King. The channel offers some excellent drifting for squid and I have seen anglers regularly take their bag limit (10) of calamari here. The most productive area is along the east side bank where there is a significant amount of seaweed growth. At times, there have been good runs of aero squid and the odd run of cuttlefish. Both make excellent bait for whiting.

Near the bottom of the channel opposite Point King, the run quickens because the channel shallows. Some big whiting have been caught here late in the ebb tide.

Sorrento Boat Moorings

During the winter months, drifting for calamari around the boat moorings is extremely productive yet their size is quite small. Still, anglers can easily yield a good catch in calm conditions. September is a great time to be working the area as the calamari size dramatically increases as the spawners arrive. This area is a known breeding ground with some calamari fetching a solid 2 kilos in weight.

Channel Marker No.1

The south western end of the Sorrento Channel is marked by a green coloured channel marker. On the southern side near the jetties, the water is quite turbulent during the ebb tide. Setting anchor and flicking squid jigs about is productive for big calamari during September and October. Garfish are also in abundance but tend to be caught in the shallower water amongst the boat moorings.

Pinnace Channel

Pinnace Channel runs along the south eastern side of Mud Island. The channel is around five meters in depth and mostly a sandy bottom which is very inviting for whiting. Throughout the summer months, angler's fishing for whiting focus on both the top and bottom sections and do very well. Some of the whiting caught here exceed 45 cm.

Mud Island

The trip to Mud Island is well worthwhile. The bottom here consists of broken ground, weed and sand areas which shelter thousands of shallow water fish like whiting, red mullet, grass whiting (strangers) and some extremely large flathead.

The island itself is flanked by the Symonds Channel on the west and the Pinnace Channel on the east. Both channels hold good snapper, flathead and salmon populations, and best fishing is the last of the ebb tide run (three hours after the reported change) and the first of the flood tide. Flounder spearing is also very popular here in the summer.

At all times when anchoring in fast tidal areas be aware of Port Rule 62A described earlier. You should also allow enough anchor rope to allow for the rise and fall of the boat caused by the wash from passing ships or swell coming through from the ocean.

In this area it is best to use a reef anchor, one that generally can be tripped and recovered. However, if the anchor becomes fouled, never be too proud to cut the anchor off and go home a few dollars shorter rather than placing yourself in a very hazardous situation.

The Great Sand at times offers some reasonable whiting catches. However due to the huge sand shifts here, the ground can change. With the use of polarised sunglasses, keen anglers can soon locate the correct area for the whiting.

Big flathead are also taken in very good numbers here and three methods are very productive. The first is to anchor in about 3 m of water and commence a berley trail. There has been success with both wet and dry berley. The cut pilchards or cubed fish method is very good and so is the pellet berley trail. Allow a half pilchard to drift back with the berley. Other anglers like spinning with diving lures like Rapalas. Another method is to free drift with bubble floats and half pilchards, fished half a metre under the float in only a metre of water. Local enthusiasts have had terrific sport with flatties up to 4 kg using this method.

Over recent years it has been proven time and again that the best way to target the flathead, especially bigger ones, is with soft plastic lures. You can either drift and cast along dropoffs or over the flats, or anchor at a chosen location and cast all around the boat.

Lower Symonds Channel

About a kilometre north of Popes Eye, the Symonds empties into the South Channel. There are some excellent days here when the lazy tide allows you to fish right through a series of tides. This

The Sorrento Channel and surrounding area is often underestimated. Calamari, garfish, flathead, salmon and silver trevally are common catches from a boat and the piers.

can only be done by studying the tide chart and recognising the neap tides. Usually the change of tide is a good time. Small pinky snapper and large whiting are the main target and they can be taken on pipis, mussels and squid. Once again, a long leader is suggested. A depth sounder is also an advantage as fishing the edges of drop-offs usually ensures some action.

Point Franklin

Within 20 meters of the rocks, the bottom is very thick with kelp beds. The tide runs extremely fast at times and the most productive fishing is up to two hours either side of the high tide. Calamari are the dominant species and can be caught with both baited jigs and size 3.0 artificial jigs.

Most of the larger sized calamari frequent the area in September although some nice models are caught throughout the winter months.

Whiting are also about in number in September but you do need to find the sand patches in order to catch them. The water is very clear so you can look over the side to find the right location to fish. Berley is essential.

Portsea Boat Moorings

South of the Portsea Pier there is a significant amount of boat moorings. Drifting throughout them is productive for calamari and if you were to anchor, flathead and whiting can be attracted with berley and caught. Fish the run out tide for best results.

Weeroona Bay

Heading a little further south past the boat moorings, Weeroona Bay tends not to see much boat traffic. There is a small sandy beach on the short and the water drops away very quickly into 17 meters of water. Along the edge of the drop there is some sea weed growth which can see some nice calamari caught when fishing the last few hours of the ebb tide.

BOAT RAMPS

There are a number of boat ramps in this section but all of them are fairly exposed and suffer from poor parking.

Mount Martha Beach: A small ramp with poor parking exposed to the weather.

Safety Beach: A concrete ramp that is exposed and again has poor parking.

Rosebud: Anthonys Nose is another concrete ramp with poor parking and is exposed in rough weather.

Tootgarook: A concrete ramp but only for small boats and again has poor parking.

Rye: The Leonard St ramp is a concrete ramp with average parking.

Rye: The ramp at the pier has good parking and can accommodate larger boats.

Rye: Tyrone Avenue can only handle small craft and has average parking.

Sorrento: The best ramp in the area with the ability to launch large craft. It is pretty well protected by a breakwall and the parking is reasonable.

SHORE BASED FISHING

Mount Martha Rocks

The rocky platform from Martha Point north to Martha Cliff is one of the best rock fishing areas in the bay. Here, within a few metres of the shore, there is 5 m of water where big snapper, flathead and gummy sharks are caught on a regular basis. Some big snapper are caught here in strong westerly and south westerlies. Fresh baits are the key and cast out as far as possible. Anglers also have great sport on skate and eagle rays, especially around Christmas. The prime position is below Bradford Road, and north to Ian Road.

Fishing for garfish from September onwards is also productive. Like all garfishing tackle, keep it light and use berley to attract them.

Huge schools of salmon frequently swim the edge of the cliffs throughout winter and early spring and if you're lucky enough to be there when they do, you can see them bust the surface in a bubbling mass. Casting metal slugs is a good method and can provide you with time light tackle entertainment, Barracouta and snook are also a common catch when spinning with metal lures.

Although there are man-made walking tracks down to the rocks it can be a dangerous trek so care must be taken. The rocks are also quite slippery so it is advisable children not be taken to this location.

Safety beach

During September, King George whiting are a common catch from the shore at Safety Beach. Fishing during dusk, anglers casting pipi baits out into the shallows tend to do quite well. The best fishing is about half way down the beach between the Safety Beach boat ramp and the entrance into Martha Cove.

Surf rods will enable a further cast but it is best when a 4–6 kg 10ft rod with a 2 oz sinker is used. The more productive whiting fishing occurs when there is a slight breeze rather than flat calm nights.

Dromana Pier

Once again, an unlikely looking pier and similar to the Seaford Pier, but one that does produce fish for the eager angler willing to work for their catch. In years past, this used to be a good night fishing spot for gars.

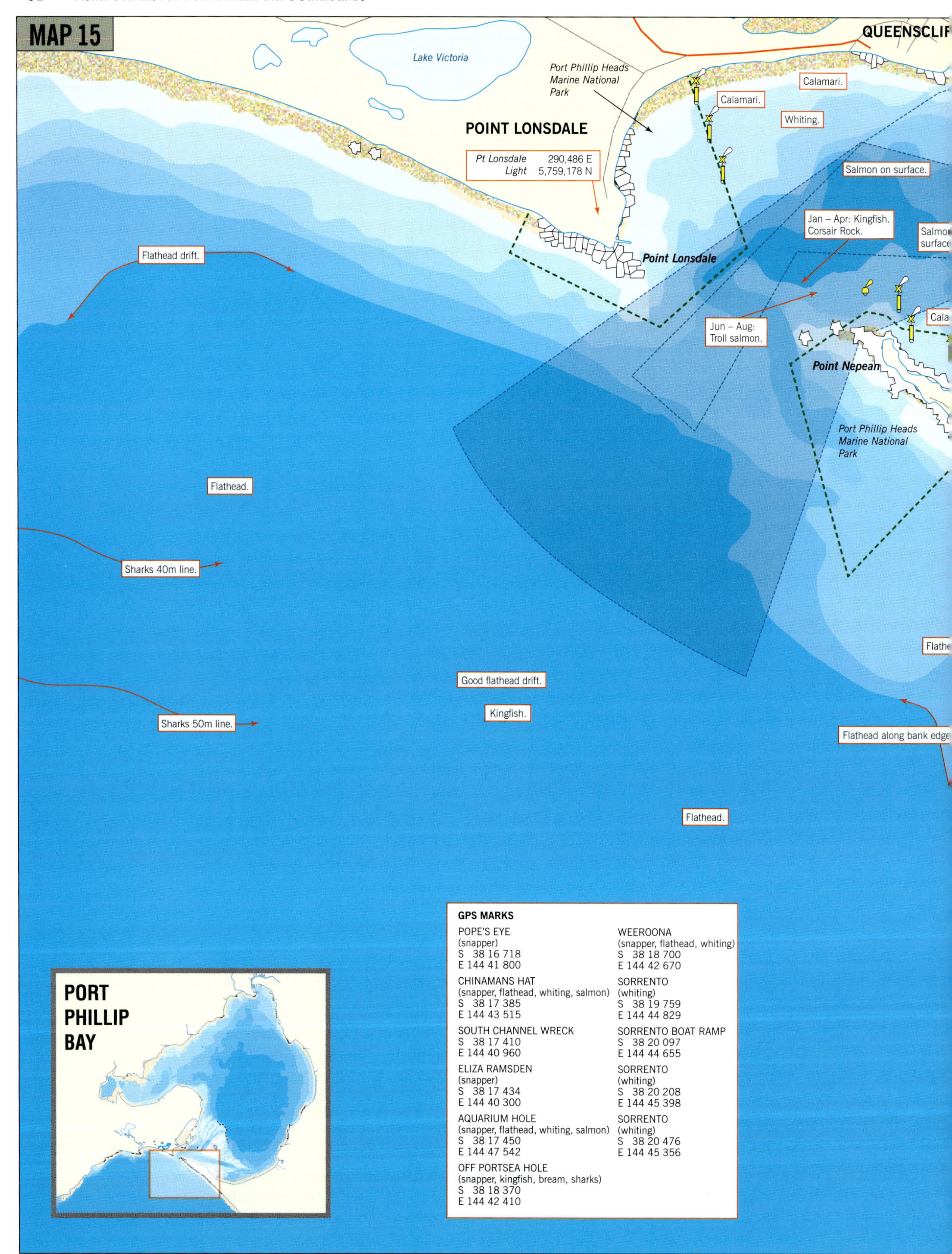
MAP 15
Lake Victoria
Port Phillip Heads Marine National Park
POINT LONSDALE
Pt Lonsdale Light 290,486 E 5,759,178 N
Calamari.
Calamari.
Whiting.
Salmon on surface.
Jan – Apr: Kingfish. Corsair Rock.
Point Lonsdale
Jun – Aug: Troll salmon.
Point Nepean
Port Phillip Heads Marine National Park
Flathead drift.
Flathead.
Sharks 40m line.
Good flathead drift.
Kingfish.
Sharks 50m line.
Flathead.
PORT PHILLIP BAY
GPS MARKS
POPE'S EYE (snapper) S 38 16 718 E 144 41 800
CHINAMANS HAT (snapper, flathead, whiting, salmon) S 38 17 385 E 144 43 515
SOUTH CHANNEL WRECK S 38 17 410 E 144 40 960
ELIZA RAMSDEN (snapper) S 38 17 434 E 144 40 300
AQUARIUM HOLE (snapper, flathead, whiting, salmon) S 38 17 450 E 144 47 542
OFF PORTSEA HOLE (snapper, kingfish, bream, sharks) S 38 18 370 E 144 42 410
WEEROONA (snapper, flathead, whiting) S 38 18 700 E 144 42 670
SORRENTO (whiting) S 38 19 759 E 144 44 829
SORRENTO BOAT RAMP S 38 20 097 E 144 44 655
SORRENTO (whiting) S 38 20 208 E 144 45 398
SORRENTO (whiting) S 38 20 476 E 144 45 356

Port Phillip Heads Marine National Park
Popes Eye
Popes Eye Bank
Spoil Ground
Mud Islands
Port Phillip Heads Marine National Park
Great Sand
Mud Island Spit
Calamari.
Kingfish.
Whiting.
Popes Eye
Chinaman's Hat
Tide Pile
Flathead on bank.
South Channel Entrance
Chinamans Hat
Good drift on soft plastics.
Whiting.
South Channel Wreck
Eliza Ramsden
Gummy sharks.
South Channel
Phillip Heads
ne National
Port Phillip Heads Marine National Park (Portsea Hole)
Off Portsea Hole
DANGER SHIPPING FAIRWAY
Recreational boat operators are prohibited from stopping, drifting, fishing or anchoring within 'transit only' zones.
NOTE: Ships may also travel outside of the designated fairway.
Gummy sharks.
ot Hill
Monash Light
Defence Road
Whiting.
Weerooma
Calamari.
Squid.
Calamari.
Gummy sharks and snapper along edge of channel.
Portsea Pier
Sorrento
PORTSEA
Back Beach Road
Franklin Road
Sand in moorings
South Sand
Calamari over weed bed.
Sorrento Boat Ramp
Garfish.
Hotham Road
Whiting.
Sorrento
Sorrento Pier
Calamari and garfish from pier.
Sorrento Channel
Sorrento
SORRENTO
Kingfish.
Calamari.
Octopus in Shark Hole.
Ocean Beach Road
Flathead.
Shark Hole
Salmon.
Sharks.
Salmon.
Calamari.
Garfish.
Flathead along bank edge.
Melbourne Road
Flathead along bank edge.
ep.
BLAIRGOWRIE
Kingfish.

Garfish are frequently caught year round. Mustad size #12 4045 ½ size hooks are the best.

In recent times, garfish have remained prevalent and a few flathead are taken from the end of the pier of an evening. Salmon or bay trout (same species) can also be caught at times when the wind is from the north.

Rosebud Pier.

This spot is a very popular pier with the kids. Flathead, pinkys, whiting, mullet and of course, gars comprise the bulk of the catch. Squid are plentiful in November and March and can be taken readily at night, with silver whiting used as bait on a jig, or on a plain colour jig during the day. The bag limit is 10 per day.

The sand holes are worth working with a mussel bait or a piece of clam for whiting and the odd big flathead that comes into the shallows toward evening.

Rosebud Pier is also know for catches of big bronze whaler sharks for those keen on a spot of heavy tackle fishing. Some of these monsters can be in excess of a 100 kilos but not regularly tackle. Only the dedicated land based angler knows when to target these monstrous animals.

Rye Pier

The Rye Pier fishes much the same as the Rosebud Pier although some anglers prefer to fish from the Rye boat ramp jetty late in the evening on a balmy summers night. Boat traffic can make fishing difficult, but if fishing late in the evening, silver trevally, garfish and calamari make an appearance often.

Rock wall at Sorrento Boat Ramp

This complex enables excellent angler access to some prime water along the edge of the Sorrento Channel. Casting baits off the end of the wall to the broken ground that lies a few metres out is well worth the effort, especially when fishing here late afternoon and early morning. You are also in with a chance of some very good whiting and plenty of squid. With a little berley, garfish are also a common catch. It is a common sight to see anglers fishing from kayak and small tinny's in search of gars.

Portsea Pier

This pier is popular with anglers and is located alongside the Portsea Hotel in Weeroona Bay. The pier itself runs into some very deep water where snapper, whiting and the odd flathead are taken. The most consistent prize and the one that makes this pier so popular is the abundant and often huge squid that move onto the broken ground surrounding the pier in late winter and spring to spawn. They can be taken by either casting a squid jig, or as most do, by putting whole silver whiting on a spike suspended under a float.

Casting a bait of pipi or fresh squid out off the pier often results in some very big whiting being taken on the last of the run in tide.

Mullet can sometimes be caught with the aid of a bread berley just at the start of the pier, in the shallows. Leatherjacket are also caught in good numbers using mussels, clams and squid for bait. Early morning is the prime time for garfish during a flood tide. Throughout the year, gars are in abundance here and the best fishing for them is on the first landing facing west. You have to get in early as it can only accommodate two anglers. Berley is essential.

The Rip

Unbeknown to the inexperienced angler, the Rip which is the entrance between Point Lonsdale and Point Nepean is very treacherous on any given day.

Ocean swells and strong tidal flows push through from Bass Strait into Port Phillip Bay and vice versa.

Many boats have sunk in the Rip over the years and it is one location not to be fished by inexperienced anglers.

Fishing here is very productive with a wide range of species on offer. Bait fishing is difficult due to the strong tidal movement and most of the time, snagging on the bottom is a common problem.

Salmon can be seen busting the surface year round and are great fun for those wanting to flick soft plastics to the bubbling mass. With all surface fishing, watch the birds dive bombing from above and you'll find the salmon. Metal slugs are also a good option as you can cast from afar to reach the fish before spooking them on the approach.

The Rip tends to attract some rather big salmon some of which can fetch 4 kg in weight.

Pike, snook and barracouta are avid lure takers and respond well to small hard body lures trolled in the localised waters. Some of the best trolling areas are along the edge of the Marine Park from Observatory Point to Point Nepean.

The Rip is also well known for kingfish which over the past few years have returned. Though not to the full extent that they were back in the glory days, kings to 15 kilos are taken each season. Fishing for them requires experience in the local area due to dangers that can arise. Kingfish are found on the bottom and when located, jigging methods yield results. Live baiting with yellow-tail scad and mackerel is the most productive method and you have to get the tides right to get baits to the bottom. Finding good grounds to catch live baits is half the battle but when you do, only take a short time to get into them before heading down in search of a king. The better areas to catch live baits from is around the Blairgowrie Marine wall and around the Portsea Pier. Berley is required to bring them on the bite.

Kingfish can be caught from December to April each year but February and March are the prime months.

Kingfish have returned and are of exceptional size in the RIP. Jigging is the preferred method used.

CHAPTER 11
PORTSEA TO CAPE SCHANCK (BACK BEACHES)
MAP 16

There are several beaches here that cater for the large number of Melbourne based anglers who love to go surf fishing—the Mornington Peninsula beaches are very popular and fortunately, very productive.

The main target is Australian salmon and the best time to fish is the top half of the flood tide. There is good fishing at all the major beaches along this stretch. Side drift can be a major problem here as huge rips occur in these treacherous waters. Use a star sinker on a paternoster rig, but on calm days, use the bomb or tear drop sinker which can drift along with the current. This is a very good way to catch fish when they are timid.

By introducing berley to the surf, you will soon attract some small mullet and salmon and then the bigger fish will follow them. The Victorian Metropolitan Angling Club won the surf competition in this area many times, and the common thread through all victories was the use of berley. Berley can be made up of many things but chook pellets soaked overnight in tuna oil works a treat.

Portsea Back Beach

This productive and easy-to-fish beach has two access points once you turn off the Nepean Highway and travel down Back Beach Road. Either turn right at London Bridge Road or continue on to the Life Saving Club. Access to the beach here is by good ramps, or at London Bridge via the sand dune. View the beach at low tide to determine where the rocky platforms and channels are and this gives a guide to where the good fishing water will be at high tide. Tides are the same as Port Phillip Heads, give or take a few minutes.

The last three hours of the flood tide and, if possible, a time when this period coincides with first light is the most productive.

A light used at night can produce outstanding results and it is wise to work a hole systematically as the fish could be schooling anywhere. If no result in 20 minutes, move to the next hole.

This is the most productive beach on the Peninsula and here the larger salmon prefer the top of the tide. The huge amounts of suspended sand can turn the fish off, however when the flood tide reaches its height the conditions normally settle.

If you fish here at night, use plenty of berley. You should also be aware that there are some big wave patterns in this area and be careful especially when wearing waders. The best times of the year here are between April and August.

Diamond Bay Back Beach

Diamond Bay isn't known as being a good fishing location but does offer some excellent fishing for silver trevally from time to time. Most of the action experienced is from April through to June. Berley is essential to bring the fish into the bay where they are known to be of respectable size. The best spot to fish is right at the bottom of the stairs as there is a sandy channel that runs between the two reefs.

When the trevally show up it is a very short period usually only lasting a week or so. Reports show that the month of January is the prime time with the best fishing on dusk during a high tide. Berley is essential to bring them within casting distance.

Rye Back Beach

This beach is either hot or cold fishing-wise. Weed can be a great nuisance and at times the surfers can also get in the way. However, despite these drawbacks, this beach still holds great fish with salmon being the main catch. Although tailor are not caught on a regular basis, two separate anglers have been seen taking tailor from here in the last 10 years. After seeing the tailor appear at the 'Warmies' in the Yarra River, the fish may well have been in transit.

Low tide shows that Rye can be very hard on sinkers, however spoon or bomb sinkers seem to escape the crevices at times. The beach fishes well in winter and the rising tide is best. The car park is right above the good fishing areas and is reached by driving down the Nepean Highway and turning down Dundas Street.

St Andrews

Few anglers fish this beach as it is off the beaten track. It is reached by travelling along the Nepean Highway to Truemans Road, then turning right down Dandy Road (unsealed), left into Bass Meadows Boulevard and from here there are many tracks leading to the beach. Like Rye, there are many rocky platforms that provide cover for the fish, much to the detriment of angler's sinkers! However, this beach does produce good mullet and salmon fishing in winter.

Best baits for salmon are whitebait, pipis and squid. Summer is a good time to try for gummy sharks mainly during the low tide when anglers can easily cast over the rocks and into the sandy deeper water beyond. The best gummy fishing is from three days lead up to the full moon and three days after.

Gunnamatta Beach.

possibly the most popular beach along the Peninsula it produces the biggest fish by far. It is a much deeper and longer beach than the others, and salmon to 4 kg have been taken. Huge hauls are very rare but unlike Portsea, where you may have 20 fish of around 300 to 400 gm, here you are likely to have 3 fish all around the 2 kg mark.

Some anglers use pilchards for bait and although productive, paternoster rigs with a pipi on one dropper and a blue bait on the other is a deadly combination. Berley works well to bring the fish into the chosen gutter being fished otherwise you'll be casting one bait into a beach that spans 18 odd kilometres in length.

There are hundreds of gutters along its length, but the deepest and most productive lies around 700 m to the left of the surf life saving club. This gutter begins at the shore and extends right out back into the ocean which is why it is so productive for salmon.

Over the last few years, spinning with metal lures has become a popular technique. Anglers focusing on the rising tide at first light do very well. Gummy sharks are also a popular target for those concentrating on fishing the lead up to the full moon. The prime months are February, March and April. It can be a very dangerous beach and anglers should study the waves before fishing. The tide here is 1 hr and 33 minutes earlier than Port Phillip Heads.

To reach Gunnamatta, drive straight down Truemans Road off the Nepean Highway until the Surf Lifesaving Club is reached.

Pulpit Rock

Some excellent catches of sweep, parrot fish and leatherjacket are taken from this platform every year. To access Pulpit Rock, park at the Cape Schank Lighthouse and follow the boardwalk to the rock ledge. The bottom is covered in heavy reef and you will lose a lot of sinkers. To avoid this, set a berley trail and fish a pilchard under a float. Salmon, barracouta, pike and snook are also a common catch when spinning with metal lures. Pinkie snapper can be taken off the bottom from September until February.

Unfortunately there is danger as in any rock fishing. Study the pattern of the waves and never fish alone. The best conditions are after a couple of days of offshore (northerly) winds.

MAP 16
Flathead.
Portsea Pier
PORTSEA
Back Beach Rd
Portsea Back Beach
Gummy sharks and snapper along edge of channel.
Calamari.
Sand in moorings
South Sand
Garfish.
Sorrento Boat Ramp
Hotham Road
Sorrento
Whiting.
Calamari on weed bed.
Calamari and garfish from pier.
Sorrento Pier
Flathead along bank edge.
Kingfish.
SORRENTO
Sorrento Channel
Calamari.
Octopus in Shark Hole
Flathead.
Ocean Beach Rd
Salmon.
Shark Hole
Sharks.
Flathead along bank edge.
Calamari.
Garfish.
Melbourne Road
Flathead along bank edge.
BLAIRGOWRIE
Diamond Bay Back Beach
Sweep.
Kingfish.
GPS MARKS
SORRENTO BOAT RAMP
S 38 20 097
E 144 44 655
SORRENTO
(WHITING)
S 38 20 208
E 144 45 398
SORRENTO
(WHITING)
S 38 20 476
E 144 45 356
N
NE
E
SE
S
SW
W
NW
0
2.5
5
Kilometres

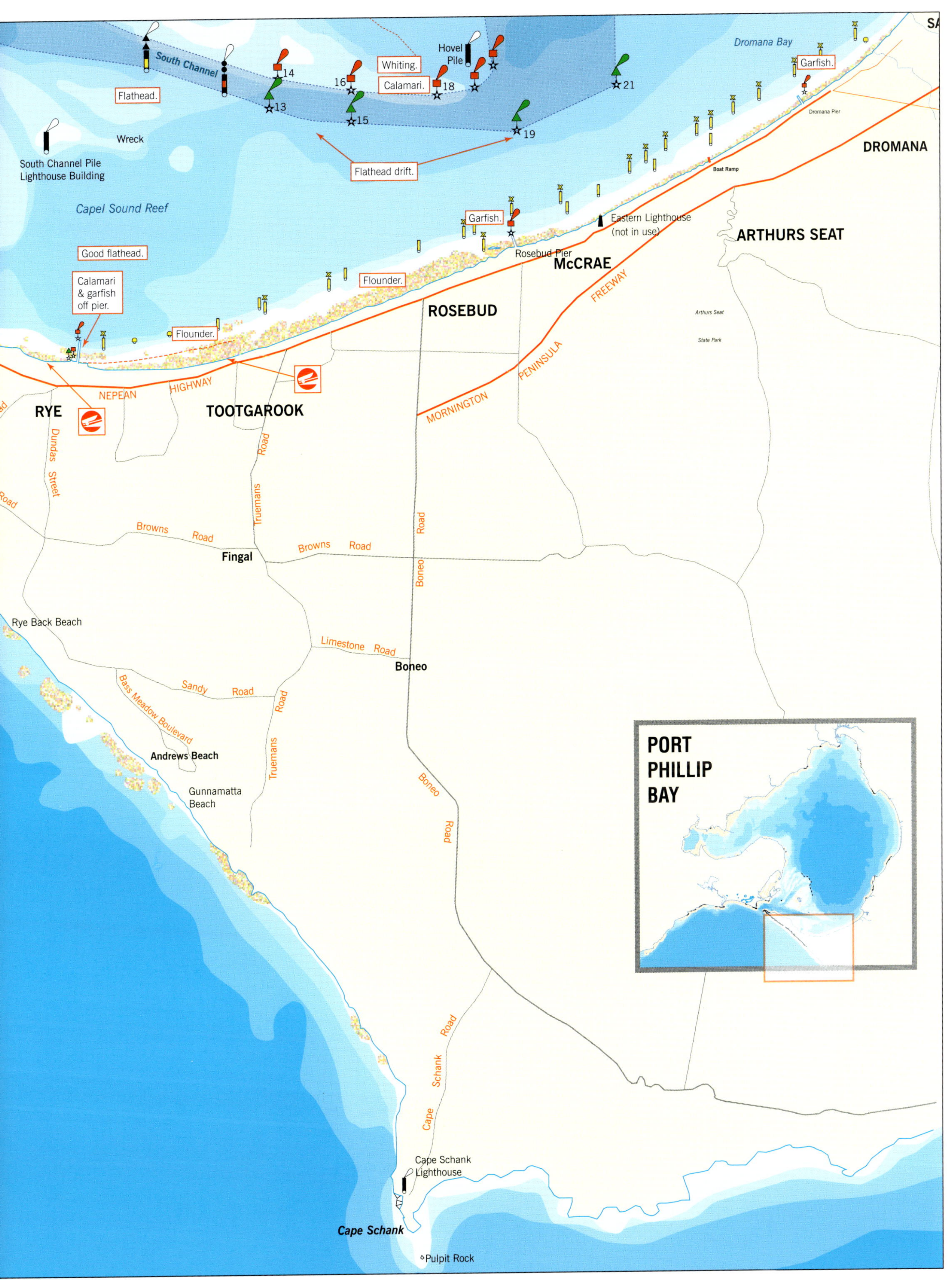
South Channel
Flathead.
Wreck
South Channel Pile Lighthouse Building
Capel Sound Reef
Good flathead.
Calamari & garfish off pier.
Flounder.
Whiting.
Calamari.
Hovel Pile
Flathead drift.
Garfish.
Dromana Bay
Garfish.
Eastern Lighthouse (not in use)
Rosebud Pier
Flounder.
13
14
15
16
18
19
21
DROMANA
ARTHURS SEAT
McCRAE
ROSEBUD
RYE
TOOTGAROOK
NEPEAN HIGHWAY
MORNINGTON PENINSULA FREEWAY
Dundas Street
Truemans Road
Browns Road
Fingal
Boneo Road
Rye Back Beach
Limestone Road
Boneo
Sandy Road
Bass Meadow Boulevard
Andrews Beach
Gunnamatta Beach
Cape Schank Road
Cape Schank Lighthouse
Cape Schank
Pulpit Rock
PORT PHILLIP BAY

PART TWO
ESTUARY FISHING

When the sun rises, estuary fishing is at its best as the fish are out searching for food.

Estuaries are simply the lower reaches of any river or creek that are subject to some tidal influence. The principle species of fish caught in estuary waters associated with Port Phillip Bay are bream, mullet, trevally and salmon. However, the occasional catch of flathead, whiting, tailor, mulloway and even pinky snapper in the lower reaches of bigger rivers such as the Yarra, does add to the list.

Coverage in this book is given to the more prominent estuaries that are the most popular fishing venues for anglers. These estuary waters include the Barwon, Werribee, Yarra, Maribyrnong and Patterson Rivers together with Balcombe Creek. Due to the complexity of each particular river system, no attempt has been made with the accompanying maps to distinguish deep water from shallow water areas.

CHAPTER 12
BARWON RIVER

The Barwon estuary consists of a narrow entrance to the sea, with minimal siltation, a broad-water extending about 2.5 km upstream from the bridge, and a long winding section of another 4 or 5 km up to Lake Connewarre.

Lake Connewarre is shallow, but there is a channel of sorts along the west side of the lake roughly joining the estuary below with the river above. Nowhere would this channel exceed 3m in depth.

Above the lake, the stretch of river to the weir is relatively deep and can be navigated in a small boat or kayak. It is very narrow and reedy, but this deep stretch of river is popular with bream anglers, most of whom have negotiated access through private property from Matthews Road.

THE MOUTH

The rocky platform under Barwon Heads Bluff on the right side of the river mouth offers some fishing platforms at low tide, both facing the ocean and in the river itself. Here, bait anglers usually encounter various species of rock fish, but of these only the blue throat tusk fish is prized. Sometimes a low tide on dusk will produce a more interesting catch including small snapper, whiting and the occasional gummy shark.

Lure casting enthusiasts who don't mind losing a lure or two in the kelp sometimes encounter large snook or long fin pike. These two species have sharp teeth so you might opt for tying on some wire between the lure and leader to prevent bite offs. Spinning with metal slugs will also catch the attention of salmon and silver trevally. The ideal lure weights range from 15 g to 35 g for this area.

Access to the bluff is from Ewing Blyth Drive then Bluff Road.

FISHERMAN'S JETTY

The Fisherman's Jetty, around which several commercial fishing vessels are moored, is a popular spot for anglers during the day, but

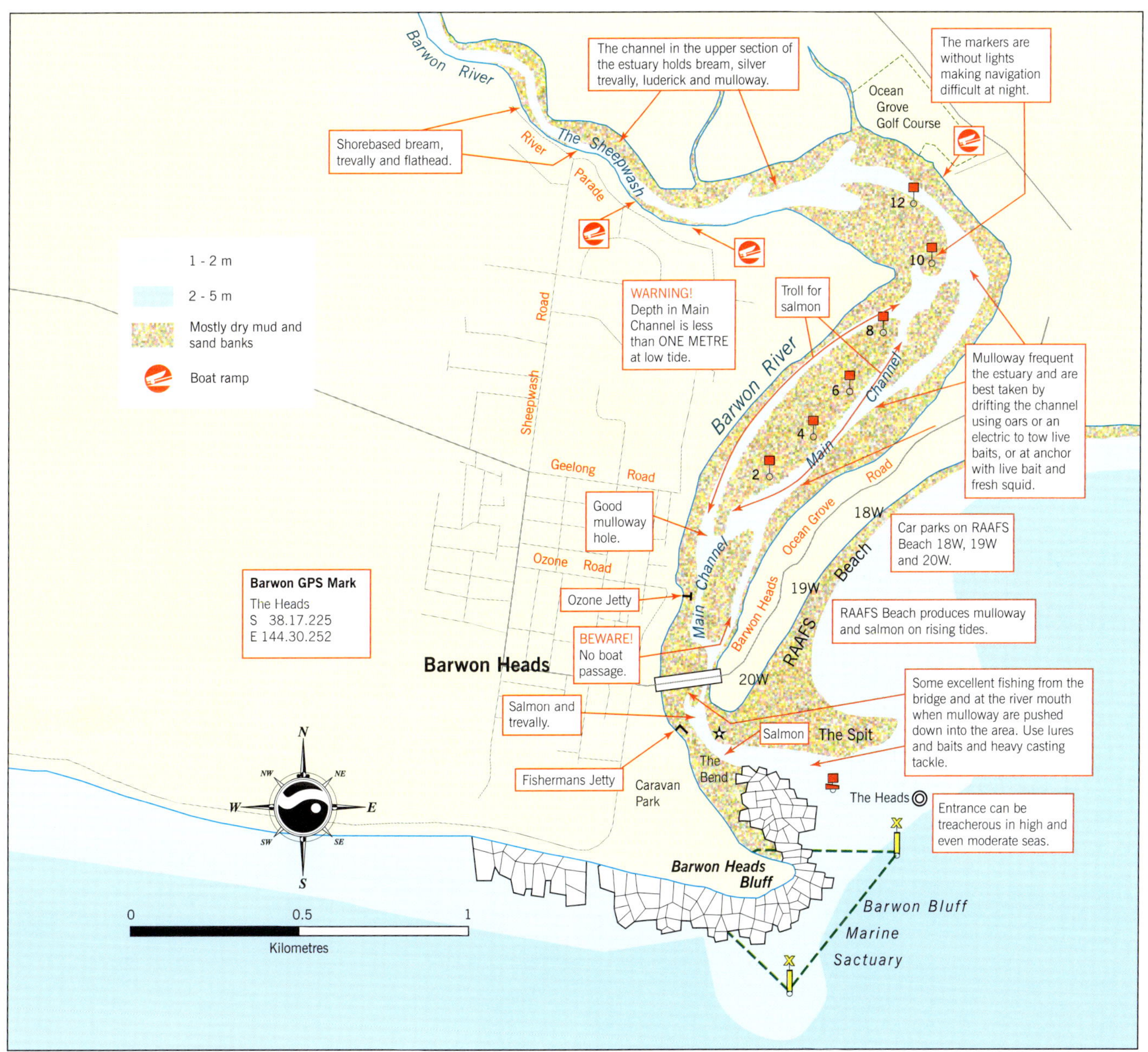

due to the extreme narrowness of the river at this point, the tides run very fast. For this reason, time your trip to coincide with the low tide change that occurs some two hours later than low water at Port Phillip Heads.

On the Fisherman's Jetty, the first couple of hours of the incoming tide will usually produce mullet and small salmon. As the tide picks up speed and the water clears, big silver trevally become a distinct possibility. The best baits for these include fresh whitebait, clams, prawns, mussels and rabbit. If you secure an onion bag full of mashed pilchards to the side of the jetty and let float on the water's surface, you'll attract fish in no time.

The steep beach downstream from the Fisherman's Jetty is also a productive spot to fish on the low tide change, with a variety of species to be caught, including mulloway when they are about.

Access to the Fisherman's Jetty is past the roundabout on Flinders Parade and then past the ranger's building in the Foreshore Caravan Park, just downstream from the bridge.

The Spit

There is a sand spit opposite the Fisherman's Jetty and a little bay back upstream toward the bridge. This is a popular spot for anglers fishing the rising tide because there is little current in the bay until the tide has covered the sand spit. There is good access to this spot from the car park on the Ocean Grove side of the bridge. It can be a great spot to berley up small mullet and salmon that can be then used as live baits to hopefully tempt a mulloway. A lot of stingrays come into this bay and they can be a nuisance on almost any tackle. There are moorings not far out in the river here, and most of the bigger rays that get hooked manage to wrap the angler's line around one of these, or sometimes a bridge pylon.

Overall this spot is not wholly negative; it is probably one of the most comfortable spots for anglers to fish the incoming current, and a wide variety of fish, including mulloway, have been caught here.

The Bridge

The bridge is a popular spot for anglers fishing for small mullet and salmon during the first two or three hours of the rising tide. Most fish seem to be caught on the Ocean Grove side of the Bridge; one favourite spot is beside the third light pole from the Ocean Grove side of the river.

The bridge draws quite a different crowd after dark, particularly in the autumn and winter when mulloway can sometimes be seen cruising up and down in the lights of the bridge as the water clears at the change of tide.

Mulloway spotting has become a regular activity with local anglers who spend hours on the bridge at night looking for a big ghostly shapes in the mercury vapour lamps of the bridge. Catching them is a different story though, for although a few are caught in the course of a season they show extreme caution when presented with bait. Most baits, even live baits, are ignored altogether.

Experience has shown that mulloway are more likely to take bait from the bridge if the water is cloudy and they can't be spotted. Under these conditions, several have been caught on lures jigged under the lights of the bridge. A red rubber octopus pattern has been responsible for several captures from the bridge under these conditions however, some have been taken on bibbed lures as well.

Watching mulloway ignore baits presented to them from the bridge makes you wonder just how often baits intended for mulloway are ignored in other parts of the river as well when the quarry is not visible.

Big mulloway seem to be most plentiful in the Barwon from March until the end of June or July and then perhaps again in November. School mulloway appear in November and December.

Ozone Jetty

This little jetty at the bottom of Ozone Road is popular with anglers and produces mullet and salmon during the first two hours of the incoming tide. Mulloway seekers fish from the Ozone Jetty with some success, the best time to get a run being from the last hour of the outgoing current until the slack water and first two hours of the incoming current. Mulloway can be quite decisive about what they choose to eat and with mullet and salmon capable of being caught here, presenting them live is the best chance at success. If you do choose to live bait for mulloway, send them out under a small

Mulloway have returned to the Barwon River system. Fishing live calamari is very successful.

bobby cork float or balloon. Mulloway fishing is best leading up to the full moon throughout the summer months.

The Mulloway Hole

At the bottom of Talbot Avenue, and between the Ozone Jetty and the creek draining the mud flats in front of the river front houses, is a popular mulloway spot. It tends to get crowded when there are a lot of fish about, and because of this, fish are lost around anchor ropes quite regularly. Live baiting salmon and mullet is the preferred and most successful fishing method.

The Broadwater

This shallow section of river between the Ocean Grove boat ramp and the bridge regularly claims the propellers of boats traveling between the ramps and the sea. The only remedy for this is to build another boat ramp downstream from the bridge.

There are a lot of small mullet and salmon in the Broadwater when they don't seem to be in the deeper stretches of the river, and boats can often be seen anchored up along here with anglers catching live bait for mulloway.

Ocean Grove Boat Ramp

The Ocean Grove boat ramp is adjacent to the car park at the bottom of Guthridge Street in Ocean Grove; toilet block and boat washing facilities are adjacent. Don't use the ramp that is in a state of collapse at the very bottom of Guthridge Street, use the one at the other end of the car park adjacent to the pontoon.

Navigation to the river mouth and back to the ramp is difficult because the water is shallow and it is rocky in many spots, particularly at low tide.

Anglers fish from the shore beside the boat ramps and good catches of mullet and small salmon are common. Silver trevally can also be caught here at times, particularly when the tide is rising.

The exposed mud flats, both upstream and down from the Ocean Grove boat ramp, are a good source of Bass yabbies for anglers equipped with pump and bucket.

The Tributary

Several creeks drain the swamp and enter the Barwon. The most substantial of these enters the river opposite the Sheepwash boat ramp, about 1 km upstream from the Ocean Grove boat ramp.

Although anglers overlook this smaller water, it is relatively deep and contains bream, luderick and some estuary perch. Bank access to this stream is limited to a swamp trail right at the bottom of Thacker Street.

The Sheepwash

Access to the Sheepwash is down Sheepwash Road, which runs off the Barwon Heads Road to the left just after you enter Barwon Heads coming from Geelong. To get to the Sheepwash boat ramp, turn right at the bottom of Sheepwash Road along the river and past the caravan park. The boat ramp is situated on the river in the fourth clearing on the left-hand side of the road.

There is enough parking for about ten cars and trailers, but no other facilities. The section of river known as 'The Sheepwash' extends upstream from the boat ramp to the third fence running to the water's edge.

The Sheepwash fishes well for bream and luderick, particularly from April to August when the weather is cold. The best time to catch these fish is during the last hour of light, particularly if the tide is running in toward full. Sand worms and locally pumped bass yabbies will take both species, and abalone gut is excellent if you are just seeking luderick.

Casting out into the middle of the river from the bank is not a good idea when the tide is running because your line just gets swept back into the bank. Putting a heavier sinker on to prevent this only makes matters worse because more weed gathers along the line before the sinker pulls.

The Thunderbolt

Upstream from the Sheepwash, between the last fence and the lake, the winding section of river is known as 'The Thunderbolt' because of the speed it can run at. There is dry weather access to the Thunderbolt from the elbow in Lake Road. Lake Road runs off the Barwon Heads Road between Connewarre and Marshmallow Road, makes a right angle bend, then runs back to the Barwon Heads Road by the Barwon Heads airfield. Never use this access if there is any suspicion of wet weather, because it winds down through the lowlands swamp to the river and often the surface is merely a crust over soft mud.

Most anglers who fish the Thunderbolt do so from boats launched at the Sheepwash. However, the majority of anglers launch boats into the river with the intention of fishing outside. There are some deep holes in the Thunderbolt area, particularly on the east side of the river and these are the places to look when there is a mild fresh running.

Lake Connewarre

Upstream from the Thunderbolt is Lake Connewarre, which covers about 1000 hectares. It is a game reserve with many water birds nesting there, ibis in particular. Motors above five horsepower are not permitted in the lake for this reason.

There are a lot of fish in Connewarre that never seem to get caught, including big sea mullet. Apart from these there are yellow-eye mullet, bream and eels. The lake is also popular with shooters in duck season and some shooters have reported sighting very large fish in the lake which would undoubtedly have been mulloway.

Landbased anglers do have access from the point at the bottom of Stacey's Road where there is about a metre and a half of water.

These days with the popularity of lure fishing, especially soft plastics, anglers in small craft such as canoes or kayaks are catching some great bream by fishing the lake, working weed and reed beds snags and any other likely looking areas.

The Second Break

The Second Break is the name of the weir across the river approximately a kilometre above the lake. Bream anglers who have negotiated access through private property to this section of the river, refer to the whole stretch between the weir and the lake as 'The Second Break'.

There is another access to the Second Break from the west arm of the lake. At the bottom of Stacey's Road there is a makeshift cutting in the bank where dinghies and canoes can be launched. From here, one can proceed north up the west arm to the opening of the river.

The entrance to the river is the second opening in the reeds on the right of the east side of the arm. It is shallow at the entrance and you might have to get out of your craft to push it over the bar, but, once inside, there is deep water—up to 3m in places.

The most sought after species here is bream, which can be taken up to a good size on a variety of baits including bass yabbies, squirters and crab. However, there are several freshwater species as well including trout, carp and redfin that come over the weir and can't get back up again.

In the past there have been a number of big brown trout caught below the weir by anglers patient enough to keep coming back until they manage to tempt one. Successful bait for these big fish is shrimp netted from the river.

In summary, the Barwon estuary is not the easiest Victorian estuary to fish, and big catches of worthwhile fish are the exception rather than the rule. The fast tides and the constant colour changes in the water drive many anglers away to fish less hostile waters.

However, the Barwon does have rewards for dedicated or specialist anglers who are prepared to spend enough time getting to know this water. Without a doubt, big mulloway are the prize fish of the Barwon, and some anglers take their share of these every year while others after years of trying, have yet to catch their first.

CHAPTER 13
WERRIBEE RIVER

This river, one of the premier bream fishing waters in the State, is like any other estuary—it carries a resident population of bream and it also receives new stocks of fish from Port Phillip Bay. The fish freshly in from the bay can be easily identified by their silvery appearance, while those that have been in the system for some time are much darker.

Although some anglers target yellow-eye mullet, small salmon, barracouta and large flathead from the river, it's the bream which are most sought after.

Baits that consistently take fish from this water are sandworms (also known as soft worms, pod worms and tubeworms), bass yabbies, squirters (soft shell), blubber worms, shrimp, peeled prawns, pipis and small freshwater yabbies.

Raw chicken is another bait that has proved very successful in and around the Port Phillip estuaries. A mixture of flour and water and made into a dough plus a pinch of curry powder then fished on small long shank hooks under a float, can produce terrific results at times.

Squirters are found on the exposed mud banks at low tide. Regulations prevent the taking of these molluscs with an instrument like a shovel or hand trowel, but they can still be gathered by hand.

Lure fishing enthusiasts yield excellent results when flicking small metal vibes and soft plastics in the river. The most productive locations are under the cliffs and around boats that are moored in the main body of the river. Working along the edge of the rock walls and weeded edges can also see some nice bream caught.

The tide in this river runs quite swiftly and the change of tide at the Barnacle Hole is about one hour after the river mouth, which in turn occurs three hours behind Port Phillip Heads.

On the Melbourne side of the river, access to the river bank for shore anglers is restricted to K Road. From there, most vantage points can be reached within easy walking distance. The Geelong side is all Melbourne Water land and a permit is required to enter. For up-to-date information about fishing access permits, visit the Melbourne Water – Western Treatment Plant website and follow the links, or phone Melbourne Water's enquiry centre on 131 722 between 8 am and 5:30 pm Monday to Friday. Permits are currently $20 for a 2 year period.

Boat anglers really have a world of estuary fishing open to them, with several inaccessible bank fishing spots reachable by boat. When the bream are found to be feeding and suddenly go off the bite, it is just a matter of moving up or down 50 m or so to find the school again. Usually the fish move up and down the estuary with the tide.

Best times for bream are October and November when spawning fish move into the river. Good fishing can also occur in winter if a decent run of fish entered the river in the previous spring.

As a rule, when there has been a run of freshwater in the river after rain, the fish tend to stick to the bottom section of the river below the Pines.

If the river is rather clean then the fish will make their way right up as far as the shallows above the pavillion. In times of very dry conditions, the fish can sometimes be found right where the mouth joins Port Phillip Bay.

Mulloway are also an option and although they are regularly caught throughout the winter months, captures are rarely reported.

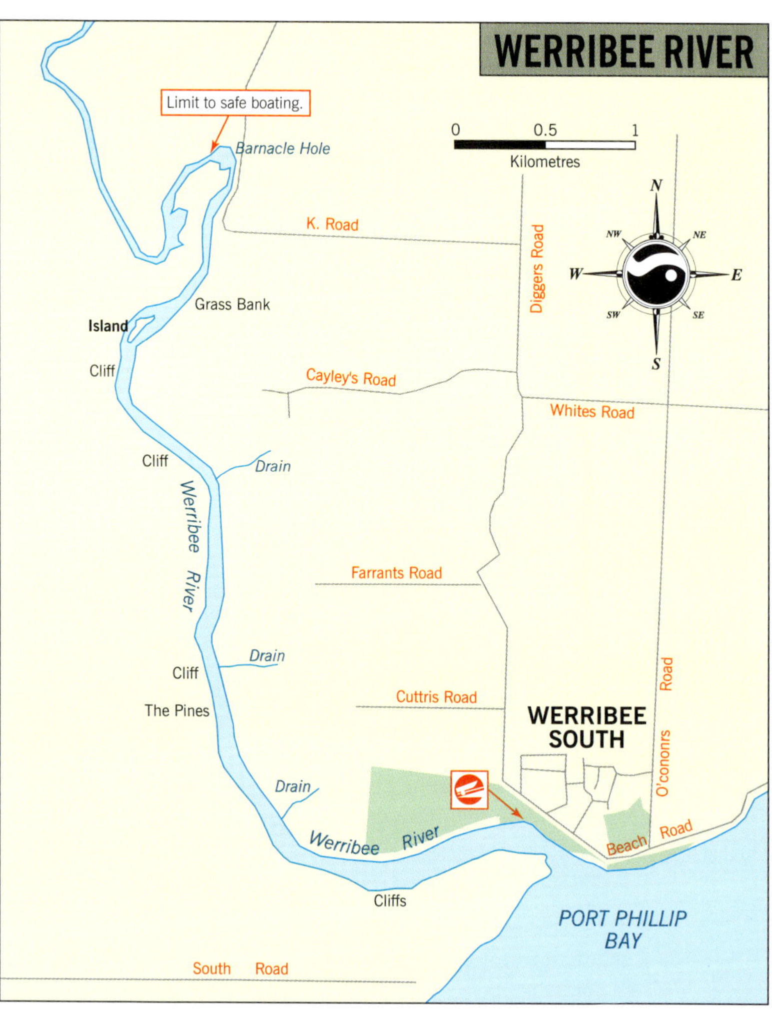

Anglers fishing for mulloway use both live baits and lures similar to that used in Patterson River.

Remember the speed limit on the river is 8 kmh.

WHERE TO FISH

CLIFFS

Careful depth sounding of this part of the river will show a large hole about 10 m deep that runs for about 50 m. When there is a lot of activity on the river, the fishing seems to be good here, and it often produces catches of big bream, particularly when using harder baits like squirters and yabbies.

THE PINES

There is a group of pine trees on the left side of the river about 2 km up from the river mouth. The fishing here is very good, however it pays to periodically check your line for abrasions from the heavy coral bed that lies here. In the past, 42 bream, all over 500 gm, have been taken here by a single angler in a Victorian Championship. Worms are great when there are no bait stealers about, and berley is useful as it seems to stick amongst the coral.

HARRISONS

This area is popular with bank anglers because it has more of a muddy bottom which allows easy fishing for mullet and medium

Bream are a common catch in the Werribee River. A great location is below the cliffs.

sized bream. Squirters are a proven bait here, particularly if small mullet are on the job with the worms. Prime shrimp can be netted along the edges in the weed banks. Weed is easily seen at low water and running a fine mesh net through the weed gives best results.

Sharkey

Good fishing is available off the bank by casting near the cliff edge that falls into very deep water. There is usually exceptional fishing from September to November when the bigger bream move upstream. Shrimps and worms are very good here. If the small mullet are on the job, try squirters and the small spider crabs found in the weed along this stretch.

Willows

The river narrows here and this area is a top spot in the spring time. Small pieces of raw chicken have at times taken fish in this area, although the ever-reliable podworm is hard to match. When the tide is flooding, allow your rig to work along the edge of the river bank which drops into quite deep channels.

Barnacle Hole

Everybody who has fished the Werribee River is familiar with this spot. For anglers in boats who do not know the area well, this area is the upper limit of safe boating water.

The Barnacle Hole usually carries good stocks of big bream but, unfortunately instances of illegal netting along here are increasing.

When fishing this spot, the best bet is to allow a small ball sinker to run right onto the hook which gives a better chance of surviving the sharp barnacles that abound in the area.

A small soldier crab fished very close to the edge here is also sometimes effective. Also really good results can be had with bass yabbies, while some regulars even use the common freshwater yabby with success.

The Shallows

This area is difficult to fish in a boat due to the shallow water and most catches are taken from the bank. Hundreds of bream are taken out of this small section at times, particularly during the months from October to November. Fishing unweighted baits like yabbies and shrimps can also be productive here.

BOAT RAMP

Werribee River: An excellent ramp in all weather condition, concrete multi ramp with plenty of parking.

Casting hard body and soft plastic lures around the moored boats can lead to some quality bream caught.

CHAPTER 14
YARRA RIVER AND MARIBYRNONG RIVER

Once heavily polluted, both rivers now run relatively clean, so with reasonable catchment health and strict controls on the material that is emptied into them, good fishing conditions should prevail.

The bottom of both rivers has always been muddy with a great deal of coral base, but the tiny micro-organisms that add so much to an estuary were totally overpowered by the pollution problem. Now that the pollution has eased, weed beds, barnacles and other marine life have regenerated, reviving reasonable fish habitat and a serious bream fishery right on Melbourne's doorstep.

The Yarra has started to fish well right up to Abbotsford, but it is the stretch between the river mouth at Williamstown and the junction with the Maribyrnong that is attracting most fish and anglers. The lower reaches of the Maribyrnong and Yarra Rivers start to fish well in June and July, prior to the fish moving upstream to spawn.

The bream come from Port Phillip Bay and most of the stocks move into the rivers from the piers around Williamstown, which include Station, Princes, Lagoon and St. Kilda Pier and Breakwall.

Around September and October, depending on the amounts of freshwater coming down from the upper reaches of these rivers, the fish start to work their way up into the spawning areas at the top of the estuary section. Both rivers have very heavy coral beds at the top of the tidal sections, and it is here that the bream spawn.

The bream schools consist of the same sexes when they are travelling to the spawning area. If you get a run of fish then they will either be all males of all females. Bream are inclined to `commit suicide' at certain times during spawning season so a reasonable bag limit placed on bream in the upper reaches of these two rivers would be appropriate.

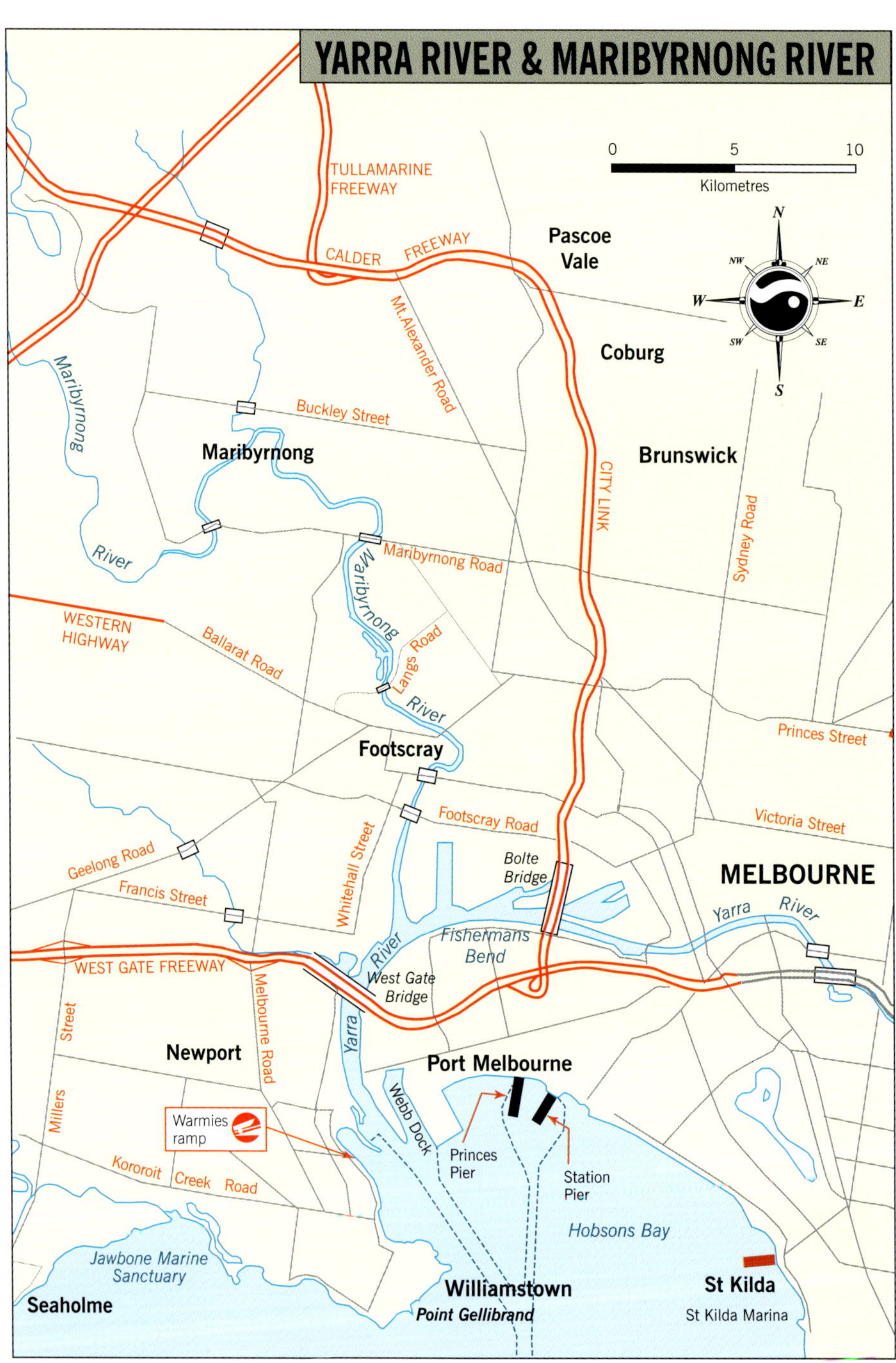

Best baits for the Yarra and Maribyrnong are bass yabbies, pod worms, shrimp, prawns (peeled or whole), crabs, squirters, raw chicken and maggots (gentles). One very productive technique has been to thread a peeled prawn onto an ultra light jig head and let it slowly freefall next to the jetty or pier pylons.

Lure fishing is also popular nowadays and with the Vic Bream Classic tournament held in the Yarra each year; more and more anglers are using these techniques. There are a multitude of jetty ruins, pylons and bridges which can be fished in the Yarra and at some point, there will be bream lurking around them.

Bream can be spooked very easily, so ensure you are being as quiet as possible. A boat fitted with an electric motor will make fishing for bream much easier. Kayak anglers certainly have the upper hand and can be launched in the CBD. Car Parking could be a problem but if you get in early enough, you find a good access point.

When flicking soft plastics, try to use the lightest weight jig head as possible such as a 1/16oz with a size 4 hook.

There is no tide preference here (like the flood at the Patterson or Werribee Rivers). As long as there is some run in the rivers, then the fish seem to take the bait well. Some areas are restricted to boats and it is an offence to anchor in the main shipping channels. There is also a speed limit of 8 kmh in both rivers.

WHERE TO FISH

Warmies (sometimes referred to as the `Hotties')

This very popular fishing spot is reached by driving to the Newport Power Station on the Geelong side of the river. The Warmies provide good fishing when warm water is coming out of the power station. Bream, mullet and tailor are the main fish taken with the odd mulloway caught at night on live mullet. As this is a popular area, there have been many rubbish bins left for the collection of refuse. Please use them in order to avoid the area being closed to anglers.

West Gate Bridge

Both sides of the river, near the pylons, fish well off the bank for bream on bass yabbies. Some nice crabs for bait can also be gathered under the rocks. A heavy sinker may be needed here when the tide is running.

Bolte Bridge

The spit of land that juts out to the middle of the bridge is a noted area for bream, and especially mulloway which hunt around here in April, May, June and July. Baits of live mullet suspended under a float are the key to these fish, and heavy tackle is required as once hooked they will try to dive back under any structure and cut you off. Cast soft plastics around the pylons from the boat. Bream are always lurking on one side of them.

River Junction

This spot is reached by walking down from Footscray Road or through Whitehall Street. Good bream, mullet and eels are often caught at the change of tide, particularly in August and September. Mulloway are often hooked and caught here on live mullet. The best time is late at night.

Footscray Road Bridge

Fish are naturally attracted to the bridge structure and many bream and mullet are caught here as a result. The stretch above the bridge and north to the Dynon Road Bridge is also a very good bream spot. Shrimp can at times be collected with the aid of a net along the retaining walls.

Langs Road Bridge

Low tide here will reveal why it is such a good fishing area. The coral and barnacle growth is amazing and it is here that some of the big bream of the Maribyrnong are taken. Bass yabbies used as bait account for some of the better catches. Fresh river shrimp, fished unweighted along the pylons are also deadly at times.

Speed restrictions apply, always pay attention.

Casting and working lures along the road bridge pylons is effective for bream and mulloway in the Yarra River.

Maribyrnong Road Bridge

Downstream from the bridge, right along the front of Fairbairn Park, is an open area that holds good bream. Large schools of mullet also move through here, and anglers using big long poles and bread dough as bait can be seen in action on most Sundays during the winter.

The Cordite

This marks the summit as far as the bream are concerned. Heavy coral areas above the bridge are where the bream are believed to spawn.

Lure Fishing

In both rivers lure fishing for bream is a very popular and effective way of catching them. The key is to use small diving lures or soft plastics and fish them near any structure, such as wharf pylons and round bridges, especially those in the Maribyrnong River. Wherever possible, cast close to structure, especially in shaded areas where the bream love to hide.

Bream are the most common catch in the Maribyrnong and Yarra rivers and can be caught using bait and lures.

CHAPTER 15
PATTERSON RIVER

This river started off as merely a drain that emptied the Dandenong and Eumemmerring Creeks into Port Phillip Bay at Carrum. With development along the Dandenong Valley in the early 1970's, effluent flowed into the system, eventually poisoning it and virtually making it dead water. Now the main floodwater is relayed down the Mordialloc Creek and most of the offending areas have been sewered.

With the large Patterson Lakes development has come marinas and huge public boat launching facilities. During the summer, thousands of craft make their way to the bay from this port. On a perfect Sunday, there would be more boats using this river to venture onto the bay than on any other waterway.

Fishing inside the river is excellent. With the improved eco-system has come the rebirth of sandworm colonies, shrimp populations and squirter beds. These three baits are the best fish producers in this system and can be collected at most vantage points in the waterway. It is wise to check with landowners before using the water around the lakes as their title or ownership includes water frontage. Although there are several restrictions, there are still plenty of areas left for fishing and one does not have to leave the main river to find fish.

Anglers fish the river mouth for mullet and bay trout (juvenile salmon). Most weekends see many anglers taking fish between the mouth and the main Nepean Highway bridge.

After flooding, the fish seem to move towards the mouth and stay well below the flow of freshwater. Best months seem to be October and November for bream, and February and March for mullet, with salmon usually turning up around Easter.

Each year the river also sees decent numbers of school mulloway move through and several anglers enjoy success chasing them with hard bodied lures or small live mullet. The best places to look for the mulloway are around any of the bridges and up towards the

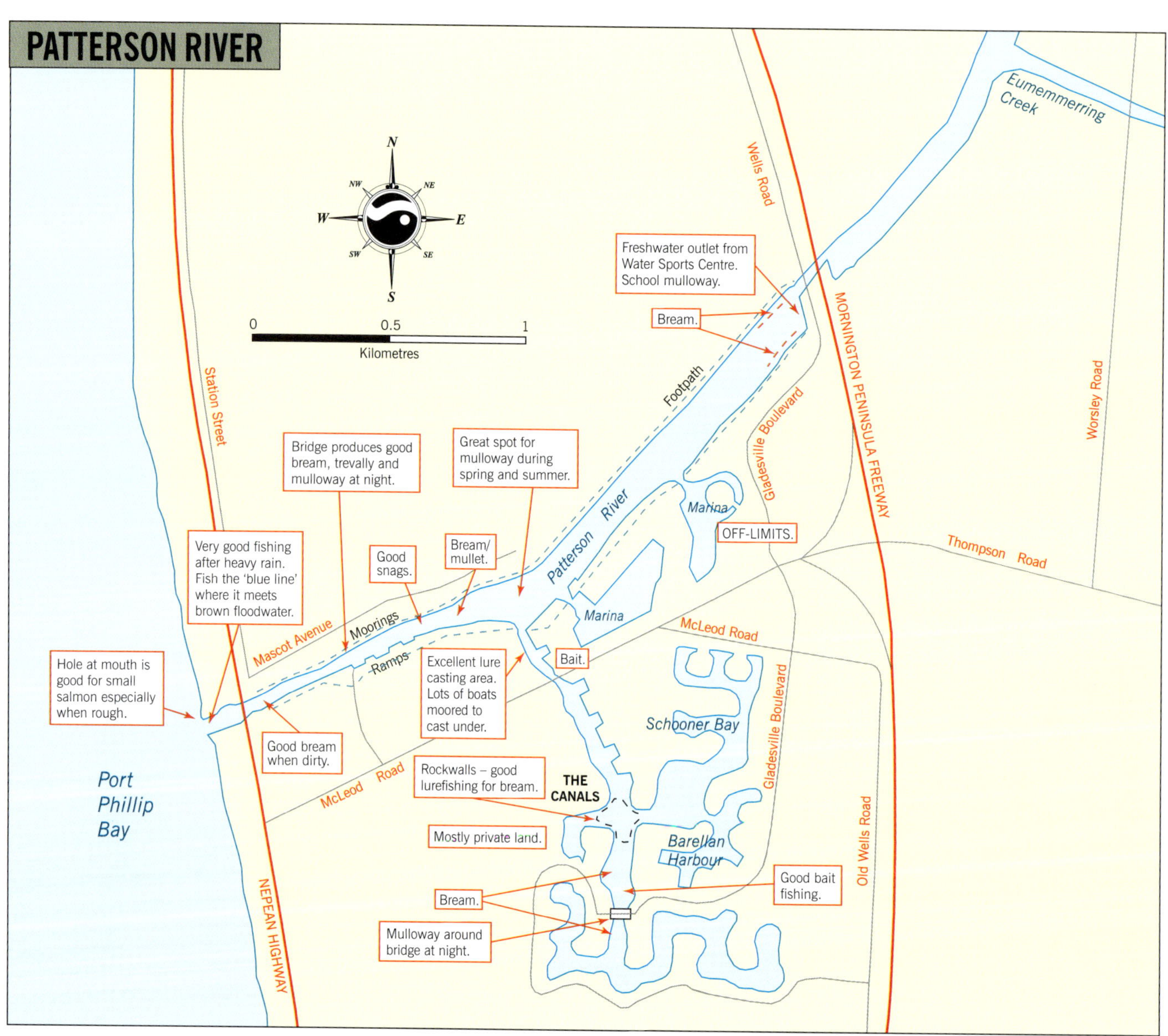

Bream feed along the rock walls, twitching lures along them is an effective technique.

Small 30 mm to 50 mm suspending hard body lures work exceptionally well on bream.

flood gates, where they will sit waiting to ambush food. February to May is a good time to find them.

Recently, estuary perch have also become a regular catch and tend to be caught around the same time as the mulloway are about. Caught as a by-catch, estuary perch can be caught when flicking soft plastics around the bridge pylons.

The river offers bank anglers great spots to try their luck but in the lakes area, a small boat is an advantage.

WHERE TO FISH

River Mouth

Good mullet and bay trout are caught here on the rising tide. During strong westerly winds, salmon can be in huge numbers in the rough conditions. When the water is clear, a small 15 gm silver lure is effective on the small salmon.

Mullet are prolific and the best baits are sandworms slowly retrieved along the bottom, or using small pieces of dough or bread about a metre under a float. Berley is an advantage and sometimes anglers pool their berley to attract and then hold the fish.

The Highway Bridge

The Highway Bridge fishes well all year and at times can support a range of species. The best fishing is during the winter months when mulloway are caught. Anglers fishing from both the right and left sides do well simply by casting soft plastics, metal vibes and diving hard body lures from one side of the river to the other.

During winter and after heavy rains, the river becomes a putrid mess of brown dirty water. Despite this flush, the bream hold up under the bridge pylons and can be caught using freshwater yabbies or earthworms. These two baits need to be fish unweighted and cast as close to the pylons as possible to entice a bite.

On the southern side of the river under the bridge, there is a small reef which juts out. At times during the year, calamari can be caught. Casting size 2.0 jigs across the river and bringing them back across the reef yields good results.

The Rocks

Situated just upstream of the railway bridge on the Frankston side of the river is an area known as 'The Rocks'. It is inclined to be very snaggy but is well worth trying a crab or shrimp bait to lure large bream away from the pylons of the railway bridge.

Good sized mullet are caught on the flood tide under a float and the odd flathead is also taken here in the summer. There is also a good supply of podworms in the general area.

Bream can be seen right throughout the Patterson River complex.

A live yellow-eye mullet fished on a 2/0 hook and running sinker rig will take some lovely sized flathead in summer and autumn.

Boat Ramp Complex

There are some very good spots along this area. Small jetties and open sand banks with some rock walls make ideal fishing spots. Good bream are taken regularly from this area when the river is at normal flow, however a flood tide is preferred. Reasonable schools of mullet are also taken here, but berley is essential. At times after Christmas, schools of trevally and small salmon move into the river and can be caught here in good numbers.

This is usually a very good area to collect shrimp, either using a trap with some fish flesh or by running a small mesh net along the retaining wall. Exercise caution however as local angler, Alan Noble, collected a tiny blue ring octopus in a shrimp net here.

Upper Reaches

This takes in the water upstream from the entrance to the lakes, right up to the Freeway Bridge. There are some very good vantage points for anglers here. Although shallow in places around the ski lane, some excellent catches of bream are taken along this stretch.

Yellow-eye mullet are also plentiful and can be caught using dough, prawn or pipi for bait. Fishing baits under a float is very productive.

At times of settled weather where there has been little fresh flow of water from upstream, the quality of the sandworms along this bank is fantastic.

CHAPTER 16
BALCOMBE CREEK

Balcombe Creek is a very small estuary in comparison to the Werribee, Yarra, Maribyrnong and Paterson Rivers. It begins its life far inland as a stream mainly from excess rain run off but with a sizeable basin nearing Port Phillip Bay. The water catchment can withstand holding a significant body of water throughout the year.

For most of the year, Balcombe Creek is closed off at the entrance which lies just under the Esplanade at Mount Martha. During a combination of heavy rains and strong Westerlies, the creek opens giving it a good flush out and if it is open for a long enough period, a new recruitment of fish enter.

The main basin is very shallow fetching only two or three feet in most parts yet still it supports quite a healthy black bream population. Though the majority of bream are small in size, fish to 40 cm are common at times.

Fishing access is mostly confined to the bank, but kayak anglers can benefit from heading up stream where fishing from the bank is impossible.

The Mouth

The mouth of the Creek is directly under the Bridge along the Esplanade. Although for most of the year it is blocked off from Port Phillip Bay, fishing under the bridge is productive for bream. It is very shallow and most of the fish can be caught right along the edges of the pylons. A running sinker rig works best with prawns a top bait.

During winter, freshwater yabbies and earth works make excellent baits.

Picnic Ground

Further up from the bridge, there is a small jetty on the southern side of the estuary. Fishing from the jetty is quite productive for bream also. The water is a little deeper in this section and float fishing is more effective. Peeled prawns make excellent baits. Larger bream can be caught along the edges.

Footy Field

Located on Seppelt Avenue there are two football ovals. You can reach the upper reaches of the Creek from behind the ovals where there is a boardwalk that runs along its length. The boardwalk provides good access to the creek but it is over grown with Tea Tree so getting a good cast can be a challenge. There are a small number of fishing platforms which can accommodate a few anglers at any one time. Freshwater yabbies make good baits in this section.

Boardwalk

A little further up from the Picnic ground a timber boardwalk runs along the edge of the creek's entirety. This provides anglers with the opportunity to fish right along the edge of the creek although due to thick timber growth, getting a good cast is hampered by the overgrowth.

Black bream are abundant along this stretch and although take they take a variety of baits, will also take lures including soft plastics.

Kayaking

Kayak anglers can certainly catch their fair share of fish and have the added advantage of accessing weed beds that are out of reach of land based anglers. Though due to the depth, manoeuvring can be difficult in some parts but in the deeper sections there will be no problem. Bream can be caught relatively easily when working the weed beds and edges. Kayakers will find that the far upper reaches can produce a larger class of fish during the summer months.

Lure fishing is also very productive.

12mm EPE foam insulation holds ice 15–24 hours

Rugged 500D PVC tarpaulin construction (10-year rated)

Heavy-duty waterproof zippers to prevent leaks and odours

Folds flat for easy storage

Perfect for boats, kayaks, utes, caravans, and camping trips

More Fish. Less Space. Built Tough

35 LITRE

OMNI - 500 mm x 400 mm x 400 mm AC9072

Total Wrap-Around Carry Handles for superior strength

Stitched and welded polyester webbing reinforcements on joins and base

Small - 750 mm x 400 mm x 330 mm

Midi - 915 mm x 460 mm x 330 mm

Small	750 mm x 400 mm x 330 mm	AC1679
Midi	915 mm x 460 mm x 330 mm	AC1136
Medium	1220 mm x 510 mm x 330 mm	AC1143
Large	1520 mm x 510 mm x 330 mm	AC1150
Extra Large	1830 mm x 510 mm x 330 mm	AC1167
Omni	500 mm x 400 mm x 400 mm	AC9072

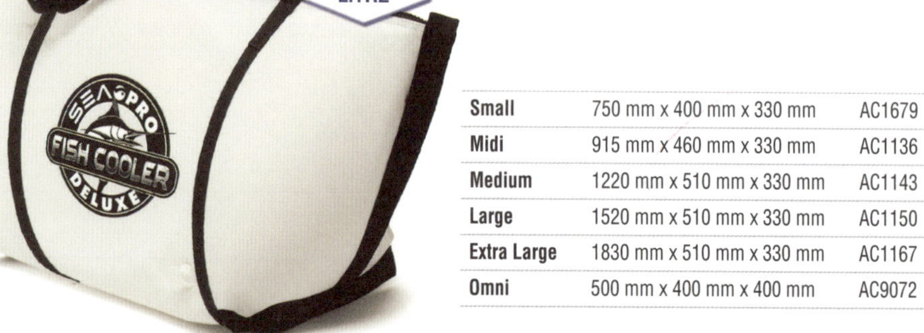

82 LITRE

Medium - 1220 mm x 510 mm x 330 mm

106 LITRE

Large - 1520 mm x 510 mm x 330 mm

- ✔ Max Volume, Min Space
- ✔ WideBase stability
- ✔ Heavy-duty 500D PVC
- ✔ 15–24 hour ice retention
- ✔ Folds flat after use

Available now — Built for Aussie anglers who demand more.

DRAIN PLUG

133 LITRE

Extra Large - 1830 mm x 510 mm x 330 mm